ARCHIVAL
STRATEGIES AND
TECHNIQUES

MICHAEL R. HILL
University of Nebraska-Lincoln

Qualitative Research Methods
Volume 31

SAGE PUBLICATIONS
International Educational and Professional Publisher
Newbury Park London New Delhi

To Mary Jo Deegan–Theorist, Methodologist, Scholar–Partner and Colleague

For information address:

SAGE Publications, Inc.
2455 Teller Road
Newbury Park, California 91320
E-mail: order@sagepub.com

SAGE Publications Ltd.
6 Bonhill Street
London EC2A 4PU
United Kingdom

SAGE Publications India Pvt. Ltd.
M-32 Market
Greater Kailash I
New Delhi 110 048 India

Printed in the United States of America

Library of Congress Cataloging-in-Publication Data

Hill, Michael R.
 Archival strategies and techniques / Michael R. Hill.
    p.   cm. — (Qualitative research methods; v. 31)
  Includes bibliographical references.
  ISBN 0-8039-4824-7 (cloth). — ISBN 0-8039-4825-5 (pbk.)
  1. Social sciences—Research—Methodology. 2. Social sciences—Archival resources. I. Title. II. Series.
 H61.275.H55   1993
 300'.72—dc20   93-11774
                                             CIP

96 97 98 99 00 01 10 9 8 7 6 5 4 3 2

Sage Production Editor: Rebecca Holland

CONTENTS

Editors' Introduction v

Acknowledgments vii

1. **Introduction** **1**
   Sociology and Biography 3
   Historians, History, and the Social Science Disciplines 4
   A Goffmanian View of Archives 5
   A Prologue to Archival Study 6

2. **Archival Sedimentation** **8**
   Primary Sedimentation 9
   Secondary Sedimentation 14
   Tertiary Sedimentation 16

3. **Structure, Control, and Technology** **20**
   Access to Archives 20
   Uniqueness of Archival Materials 22
   Noncirculating Materials and Spatiotemporal Constraints 23
   Property Rights 23
   Closed Stacks 24
   Technology and Control 25

4. **Getting Started: "Targets" and "Tool Kits"** **27**
   Names and Archival Research: Naming a Target 27
   Compiling Archival Tool Kits 28
   The Name-Oriented Search for Archival Collections 33
   Alternate Search Strategies 36
   Contacts to Make Before You Visit an Archive 38

5. **Orientation Interviews** **41**

6. **Confronting the "Black Box" Problem** **44**
   The General Catalog 45
   Finding Aids 46

Seeking the Archivist's Advice 47
Confronting and Minimizing Archival Errors:
    Type II and Type I 48
Summary 49

7. **Life in the Reading Room** **50**
Reading Room Protocols 52
Making and Reading Photocopies 54
Reading Microfilms 55
Archiving at a Distance 56

8. **Strategies for Organizing Archival Data** **58**
Spatiotemporal Chronologies 59
Networks and Cohorts 61
Backstage Perspectives and Processes 62

9. **Methodological Complexities** **64**
Getting Caught in the Concrete 64
Multiple Communications 66
Knowledge and Iteration 67
Strangers to the Past 68
Fabrication and Vulnerability 68

10. **Publication, Citations, and Permissions** **69**

11. **Nonarchival Data Sources** **73**
Example 1: Reconstructed Libraries 75
Example 2: Public Speaking Engagements 76
Summary 77

**Appendix: Epistemology and the Search
for Unsung Social Scientists:
A Rationale and Pragmatic Strategies** **78**

References **82**

About the Author **88**

EDITORS' INTRODUCTION

"Taking history seriously" is now a common social science aphorism. Increasingly, social science writings—monographs, articles, theses—contain historical data and analysis. It seems that making sense of the "raw bunch of occurrences" that constitute history or, at least, unmade history is becoming a skill to be appreciated and cultivated by social researchers of many kinds. Sociologists, for instance, look to the temporal development of institutional forms as well as to the emergence over time of particular social practices and concepts. Anthropologists, too, trace historical shifts in communities or cultures and must often study records as the collective memory of a specific people. Although the relevance of archival work is beyond question, how such work is accomplished has not been given much attention by social researchers trained outside the humanities.

This is a shame because there is a good deal to learn. Yet many social researchers—veterans and wanna-bes alike—think of archival research as a variant of library work. It is treated as a documentary rather than a discovery process. To do history then is merely to march off to the appropriate library, examine what is on the shelves, take careful notes, and, after exhausting the stacks, write up what one learned. Such work demands patience and the ability to pose good questions, of course, but the conventional wisdom holds that creativity is limited in such projects and that method is more a matter of staying awake than making intelligent choices. Given such a framework, the status of sociohistorical work suffers and a misleading characterization of archival research develops, making it appear tedious if not routine. Compared to other types of social research, archival techniques seem unexciting and dull.

Michael R. Hill, in the 31st volume of the Sage Qualitative Research Methods Series, is out to challenge and alter this perspective. *Archival Strategies and Techniques* is a call to improve and increase the use of historical records in social research—in particular, the use of those unique, noncirculating records found in special collections. This call is accompanied by a most practical and detailed guide for how original archival research can be accomplished with quality and dispatch. Such practical advice is welcome and persuasive because Professor Hill brings to this monograph extensive firsthand experience with archival research. The writing is thus informed by a solid ethnographic understanding of what shapes "life in the reading room" (among the "stack rats").

The result is a skillful blend of contextual description and methodological advice. Such a mix is necessary because archival settings and materials are unfamiliar to so many social researchers. To understand, for example, the importance of what Hill calls "orientation interviews" requires knowing something about the professional culture of archivists and the near absolute power they exercise in their domain. Or, more critical perhaps, to usefully interpret archival materials requires an appreciation for the way such materials enter the archive in the first place (what Hill calls "sedimentation practices"). In the end, Michael R. Hill not only invites us to take history seriously but shows us that archival work can and should be as innovative, engaging, and consequential as any form of social research. On to the archives.

John Van Maanen
Peter K. Manning
Marc L. Miller

ACKNOWLEDGMENTS

All scholarly expression necessarily follows in others' footsteps. I am indebted centrally to the theoretical, sociological, and archival insights of my life-partner, Mary Jo Deegan. She introduced me to Goffman's (1974) *Frame Analysis* and I learned much of what I know about archives from working literally at her elbow. I am grateful for her laserlike reading of the manuscript, but refuse her suggestion to curtail my references to her published work. Several savvy archivists and their associates showed me the ropes, often behind the scenes, including Lynn Beideck-Porn, Richard B. Bickel, Connie L. Cartledge, James Cassedy, Paul I. Chestnut, Janet Hargate, Kevin B. Leonard, Linda Long, Judith W. Mellins, Daniel Meyer, Earl M. Rogers, Charlotte W. Smith, Susan Stead, Joseph G. Svoboda, David Wigdor, and Ronald S. Wilkinson. To Erving Goffman, who is probably busy stage managing the Elvis sightings, I telegraph my deep respect.

The manuscript in various versions benefits from the direct input of Mitch Allen, Alan Booth, Miguel Carranza, Marc L. Miller, Robert H. Stoddard, and John Van Maanen. Shulamit Reinharz encourages my interest in archives. Gary Alan Fine enlivens my penchant for Goffman. Early versions of my ideas aired in papers delivered to the Association for Humanist Sociology (Hill, 1989a) and the American Sociological Association (Hill, 1990b). For a sobering introduction to the *realpolitik* of disciplinary infighting over archival control, I must acknowledge my official stint on the ASA Ad Hoc Committee on Archives. For useful questions, I thank the participants in the archival workshops I conducted for the Association for Humanist Sociology and the Midwest Sociological Society in 1991 and 1992, respectively. For friendly smiles, my blessings to Joleen Deats, Marilyn Hitz, and Roxann Roggenkamp.

My trips to distant archives were facilitated by an Alice Frost Howard Fellowship and a Maude Hammond Fling Dissertation Travel Award (both granted by the University of Nebraska-Lincoln), an award from the Talcott Parsons Memorial Fund at Harvard University, an ASA/NSF Problems of the Discipline Grant from the American Sociological Association (allowing me to spend two months at the Library of Congress arranging the then uncataloged papers of the American Sociological Association), and a Travel to Collections Grant from the U.S. National Endowment for the Humanities (permitting a month of study at Stanford University).

The suggestions in this book are based on participant observations conducted over the last five years during hundreds of research hours in archives large and small, including: Special Collections Department, Leland Stanford Jr. University, Stanford, CA; Manuscript Division, U.S. Library of Congress, Washington, DC; Roscoe Pound Library, Association of Trial Lawyers of America, Washington, DC; Moorland-Spingarn Research Center, Howard University, Washington, DC; U.S. National Archives and Records Administration, Washington, DC; Herbert Hoover Presidential Library, U.S. National Archives and Records Administration, West Branch, IA; University Archives, University of Iowa, Iowa City, IA; Chicago Historical Society, Chicago, IL; Special Collections, Joseph Regenstein Library, University of Chicago, Chicago, IL; Special Collections, University of Illinois at Chicago, Chicago, IL; University Archives, Northwestern University, Evanston, IL; Schlesinger Library, Radcliffe College, Cambridge, MA; Special Collections, Harvard Law School Library, Harvard University, Cambridge, MA; University Archives, Pusey Library, Harvard University, Cambridge, MA; U.S. National Archives and Records Administration, Suitland, MD; College Archives, Kalamazoo College, Kalamazoo, MI; House of David Collection, Benton Harbor Public Library, Benton Harbor, MI; University Archives, University of Nebraska-Lincoln, Lincoln, NE; Nebraska State Historical Society, Lincoln, NE; University Archives, Miami University, Oxford, OH; and State Historical Society of Wisconsin, Madison, WI. Visits to foreign facilities include National Archives of Canada, Ottawa, Canada; and Manuscripts Room, University College London, London, United Kingdom.

Finally, Emma, who wagged her tail, played ball, and begged for cookies throughout the writing of this book, was more help than a dog can know.

ARCHIVAL STRATEGIES AND TECHNIQUES

MICHAEL R. HILL
University of Nebraska-Lincoln

1. INTRODUCTION

Social scientists who use archives enter a new world of information. These repositories challenge and extend the usual methods of finding and collecting data. The special interests and needs of the social sciences require an introduction to archives that specifically encourages our collective sociological imagination. This book outlines the disciplinary, social, and structural contexts of archival materials (Chapters 1-3), details the preliminary work required before visiting an archive (Chapter 4), explains what to do upon arrival at an archive (Chapters 5-7), and suggests basic ways to organize and reference what you find in archives (Chapters 8-10). Finally, there is a brief guide to useful nonarchival data sources (Chapter 11).

I offer several strategies and techniques for recovering data from archival repositories for the purpose of sociobiographical and sociohistorical analyses in the social sciences. In practice, the realities of archival investigation are not so neatly packaged as the chapter headings herein suggest. Skilled archival researchers will smile knowingly at what can only be a summary introduction to the knotty sociohistorical riddles that can so easily define, if not consume, entire scholarly careers. Thus, a disclaimer is warranted.

My primary caveat is that I intend this book for students and social scientists with little experience in archival research. Novice gumshoes will learn something herein, whereas accomplished sleuths may be disappointed.[1] Advanced readers should note also that I do not address the problems of quantitative research in archives or the processing of "archived" statistical data.[2] Using census tapes and related statistical files typically involves an "archival" retrieval dimension, but pursuing that theme takes us in very different operational and conceptual directions than does the sociohistorical use of manuscript repositories, the focus of this monograph.

The major bias in this book is toward disciplinary sociobiography[3]—that is, using intersubjectively verifiable archival data to document and explicate the lives, ideas, intellectual accomplishments, and institutional embeddedness of our predecessors in the social sciences.[4] My emphasis—and many of my examples—will hopefully nudge readers toward the joys and complexities of using manuscript repositories as empirical anchors for reconstructing disciplinary history. Fortunately, many of the suggestions in this book apply equally to studies of social movements, formal organizations, and institutional processes—at least to the extent that these phenomena leave evidentiary traces in the nation's archives.

An important starting point for sociohistorical research is to inventory the myriad institutional processes in which persons, organizations, or social movements become institutionally ensnared—thus producing the residual traces found in archives. Harriet Martineau (1838/1989), author of the first major treatise on sociological methodology, wisely advised paying careful attention to the cultural and material residue of institutional processes—and her recommendation is no less relevant today (Hill, 1989b). The institutional fabric of modern societies captures traces of individuals, organizations, and social movements in a variety of complex ways, including physical traces collected in cultural monuments such as libraries, museums, and formal archives.

This volume is concerned principally with the tangible, intersubjectively verifiable trace evidence found in formal archives. Formal archives are operationally defined here as the thousands of archival facilities listed in the *Directory of Archives and Manuscript Repositories in the United States* (National Historical Publications and Records Commission, 1988).[5] These facilities are storehouses of rare, often unique materials that were created over time by individuals, organizations, and social movements.

Such materials include letters, diaries, confidential memos, lecture notes, transcripts, rough drafts, unpublished manuscripts, and other personal and organizational records. The range of materials discovered in archives can be surprising, especially in repositories maintained by colleges and universities (Brichford, 1980, p. 455).[6] Such materials are traces of past human activities (Webb, Campbell, Schwartz, & Sechrest, 1966) and they provide data useful to sociohistorical research.[7]

Sociohistorical research, by which I mean historical investigation informed by social scientific perspectives, is a venerable tradition. Many celebrated sociologists[8] embraced intellectually the great temporal sweep of institutionalized social patterns. C. Wright Mills (1959) asserted the necessity for historical perspective in all sociology, and Anthony Giddens (1987), a leading theorist of our hypermodern age, argued convincingly for renewed focus on the historical aspects of social problems and institutional patterns.

Emphasis on historical perspective supplemented by archival data is alive and well in recent sociological scholarship. For example, Aldon Morris (1984) analyzes the origins of the civil rights movement. John Stanfield (1985) documents the effects of Jim Crow law and ideology on the work and ideas of Afro-American social scientists. He reveals how previous accounts of the history of the social sciences hide a racist infrastructure of knowledge and practice. Jill Quadagno (1988) traces the transformation of the U.S. old age security program during the 20th century. Mary Jo Deegan (1988a)—in a paradigm example of data collection by a sociologist using multiple manuscript repositories—radically challenges the status quo by critically reconstructing the historical and institutional foundations of American sociology. It is with this potential firmly in mind that this book pays special attention to the social and institutionalized aspects of the data of biography.

Sociology and Biography

Individual biography cannot be grasped adequately outside of a sociological framework. C. Wright Mills (1959) put it thus: "We have come to see that the biographies of men and women, the kinds of individuals they variously become, cannot be understood without reference to the historical structures in which the milieux of their everyday life are organized" (p. 158). The relationship between society and biography is dynamic, reflexive, and interconnected.

Many apparently idiosyncratic actions are deeply embedded in institutional structures: "Individuals perform discrete institutionalized actions within the context of their biography" (Berger & Luckmann, 1966, p. 65). Institutional patterns (the core subject matter of sociology) are inextricably rooted in the everyday biographies of individual participants in social activities. As institutions are fundamental to understanding an individual life, the study of individual biographies opens institutional patterns for scrutiny—and change.

Biography is a surprisingly familiar format in sociology. One of the earliest sociologists, Harriet Martineau (1869), wrote biographies, primarily of people known to her in a variety of disciplines. More typically, however, sociologists write intellectual biographies of other sociologists, particularly theorists.[9] Biographical "life history" documents have been staple data sources for sociology ever since Thomas and Znaniecki (1918-1920) published their landmark study on the Polish peasant. The intellectual lives of sociologist scholars thematically unify the content of countless theory books and "origins of sociology" chapters in introductory textbooks. Every literature review presents the life history of a set of ideas. Intellectual biography, explicitly or implicitly, is integral to most projects in the social sciences. Advanced readers should note that Norm Denzin (1989) provides a sociological elaboration on the theory of biography in an earlier volume of the Sage Qualitative Research Methods Series.

Historians, History, and the Social Science Disciplines

It is a mistake to leave historical analyses of the social sciences to professional historians.[10] Historians, as disciplinary outsiders to the social sciences, typically do not understand our intellectual and organizational projects. Most historians frame and answer questions such that many core issues important to the social sciences are either poorly addressed or ignored altogether.[11] In order to recover our own disciplinary history and advance our intellectual understanding of past events, social scientists must learn to use the materials that historians have staked out traditionally as their own.

The distortions in the historical reconstruction of the social sciences cannot all be laid at the door of historians, however. Numerous social scientists have contributed misrepresentations of their own, albeit with different substantive aims, political agendas, and disciplinary blind spots.

The biographies of social scientists written from privileged, interior disciplinary vantage points rely too often and too heavily on apocryphal anecdotes, student recollections, and the eulogies of esteemed colleagues. It is here, as social scientists, that we can learn from our co-workers in departments of history. The classical model of patient, systematic, carefully documented historical research offers much for social scientists to respect and emulate.

Excavating the unknown, the unwritten, or the unrecognized in the history of the social sciences requires reversing the conventional wisdom of social research. The inherent liminality of such a strategy makes it suspect to those who do not appreciate the playful element in scientific research (Turner, 1969; Deegan & Hill, 1991a). Researchers should be fun-loving, as John Dewey (1913) observed: "Much, if not all, of what is termed the love of truth for truth's sake in scientific inquiry represents the attitude of play carried over into enjoyment of the activities of inquiry for its own sake" (p. 727). The playful element here is the irreverent phenomenological bracketing of one's presuppositions as to who is and who is not a relevant social scientist, or what is or is not a relevant or important topic. We look not to where centripetal citation studies and literature searches reveal a feast of prior studies. Rather, we search playfully in the opposite directions, to where conventional wisdom predicts a famine.

It should be clearly understood that purposefully looking for unsung social scientists requires patience and "the long view" (see Appendix). Many investigators are reluctant to settle for "negative findings" in the short term, but such projects cannot be rushed. David Riesman (1962) once observed that most sociologists "are unwilling to do what the physical scientists take for granted, namely, to undertake work that has very little chance of producing positive results, and then to report any negative findings" (pp. 54-55). Eschewing "quick and dirty" formulas or a "sure bet" publication opportunity is risky in terms of instant payoff, but patient, creative, and intellectually significant scholarship is inherently more satisfying (Deegan & Hill, 1991a).

A Goffmanian View of Archives

It is a *working hypothesis*[12] in this volume that archival projects are embedded in standing institutional patterns and practices, and therefore that social scientists are well positioned to recognize the social context of archives and make theoretical sense of archival activities. To this end, I adopt Erving Goffman's dramaturgical perspective and his comprehensive metatheory of meaning (i.e., frame analysis) to provide an interdisciplinary vocabulary for talking about "framing," "presentations of self," archival "performances," "interaction rituals," and the "front" and "back" regions of archives; for conceptualizing "fabrications" in archives; and for hypothesizing working responses to Goffman's general frame analytic question, "What is going on here?" Much that "makes sense" in this volume rests on Goffman's (1959, 1967, 1974) extraordinary shoulders.

Activities in archives, it will be seen, are not wholly systematic "guided doings." The absorbed scholarly calm and the ordered, professional serenity of a well-appointed archival reading room can camouflage a variety of curious activities. Using Goffman's (1974) categories of meaning, these include: archival muffings (e.g., misfiled, mislabeled materials), archival stunts (e.g., thefts of well-guarded materials), astounding complexes (e.g., discovering "bizarre" materials in otherwise "understandable" collections, an event usually marked by an archivist's announcement: "I can't imagine where this came from!"), and fortuitous discovery (e.g., finding useful materials in unlikely files). Nonetheless, my problem as an author is to provide some sense of systematic coherence in the process of archival research for sociohistorical investigations, hence the following chapters.[13]

A Prologue to Archival Study

My guiding understanding of archival work goes something like this: In archival work, what you find determines what you can analyze, and what you analyze structures what you look for in archival collections. This is blatantly circular—and points to the necessarily provisional and iterative essence of ongoing archival work. Investigations in archives simply cannot be predicted or neatly packaged in methodological formulas that guarantee publishable results. That for me is an attraction, but to others it may seem too indeterminate, too risky.

Archival work appears bookish and commonplace to the uninitiated, but this mundane simplicity is deceptive. It bears repeating that events and materials in archives are not always what they seem on the surface. There are perpetual surprises, intrigues, and apprehensions. Archival research holds the power to confirm as well as to disturb our collective legitimations. Archival discoveries are, often as not, threatening to established reputations and the hegemony of the status quo. Archival work is never the safe road, because we know not where it leads—or who may want to lead us in one direction rather than another. Visitors to the archival past should never forget, as Goffman reminded us, that we can never really know when we are being duped by others—or by ourselves.

The great puzzlement, as Goffman saw it, is to understand how people get on with life while living with the absolute structural certainty that the epistemological rug can be pulled out from under us at any moment— as it is occasionally. This book offers techniques for "getting on" with archival research for sociohistorical and biographical purposes while pointing out that archival study, embedded as it is in everyday social life, is rife with opportunities for deceptions and misconceptions.

I have, unfortunately, very little room to write about the genuine excitements and lasting personal rewards of archival work. Suffice it to say that it is a rare treat to visit an archive, to hold in one's hands the priceless and irreplaceable documents of our unfolding human drama. Each new box of archival material presents opportunities for discovery as well as obligations to treat the subjects of your sociobiographical research with candor, theoretical sophistication, and a sense of fair play. Each archival visit is a journey into an unknown realm that rewards its visitors with challenging puzzles and unexpected revelations. As a social scientist who looks archivally toward the past, you can give us new understandings of our society and our disciplines that will take us with greater clarity and equanimity into our collective future.

NOTES

1. Readers with demands greater than can be addressed in this volume can consult with profit: Brooks (1969); Duckett (1975); Kenworthy, King, Ruwell, and Van Houten (1985); Larsen (1988); Platt (1981a, 1981b); and Stanfield (1987).

2. Preliminary attempts to unite quantitative and qualitative perspectives with respect to archival data in sociology include the Griffin and Quadagno (1988) ASA didactic seminar which focused in part on analyses of records maintained by the U.S. National Archives and Records Administration. A new and growing phenomenon that future editions of this book must eventually address is the increasing utilization of electronic communications media within our intellectual and bureaucratic worlds.

3. Judy Long (1987) gives particular vibrancy to the term *sociobiography* and provides insight into how such studies illuminate the lives of women.

4. For examples of my own approaches to sociobiographical research, see Hill (1981, 1984, 1988b, 1988c, 1989a, 1989b, 1989c, 1989d, 1989e, 1990a, 1990b, 1991, 1992, forthcoming); Hill and Deegan (1991); Deegan and Hill (1987, 1988, 1991a, 1991b, 1999c, 1991d).

5. Although many of the suggestions in this book apply to research outside the United States, access to foreign archives depends much more on making advance contacts, obtaining government or other official approval, demonstrating proficiency in relevant foreign languages, and possession of a healthy travel budget. Consult your reference librarian to locate published guides to foreign archives. For an excellent example of such handbooks, see Foster and Sheppard's (1982) useful manual on archives in the United Kingdom. Also, consult the 10-volume *Index of Manuscripts in the British Library* (published by Chadwyck-Healey in 1984).

6. For example, a partial sample of eclectic materials encountered in my own archival visits includes: advertising handbills, architectural models, athletic gear, lantern slides, loving cups, maps, medals, military uniforms, oil paintings, passports, photograph albums, plant specimens, posters, rare books, stereopticons, stuffed animals, tape recordings, ticket stubs, visiting cards, and so on.

7. It should be noted that sociologist Jennifer Platt (1981a) observes—in an essay specifically on using documentary data—that sociologists do not often work the kinds of handwritten primary sources that historians routinely consult. This situation is rapidly changing.

8. For example, H. Martineau (1848, 1864), K. Marx (1867/1906), W. E. B. DuBois (1899), G. E. Howard (1904), M. Weber (1958, 1968, 1985), J. Addams (1916), and G. H. Mead (1936).

9. See, for example, Abbott (1939, 1950), Hammond (1964), Balander (1974), Blackwell and Janowitz (1974), Horowitz (1983), or Deegan (1981, 1988a, 1991).

10. The important question of where to classify history and the social sciences in relationship to the sciences, the humanities, and their interdisciplinary interstices is here skimmed over for the didactic purpose of emphasizing differences rather than similarities. There are a few historians who are properly called social scientists just as there are occasional social scientists who do justice to the title historian.

11. Dorothy Ross's (1990) *The Origins of American Social Science* is an instructive example of how a historian bent on propping up a pet hypothesis (i.e., "exceptionalism") tendentiously distorts the history of American sociology in the process.

12. The notion of a *working hypothesis* is a symbolic interactionist concept developed sociologically by George Herbert Mead (1899) and usefully brought up to date by Deegan (1987b).

13. My task is similar to that of a lecturer who, to be successful at lecturing, must present a monologue such that the audience goes away feeling that something worthwhile has been said (Goffman, 1981).

2. ARCHIVAL SEDIMENTATION

The routes by which materials come to repose in archives are neither certain nor systematic. Researchers who understand this situation stand a much better prospect of successfully unearthing archival gold. They also confront more calmly the frustrating gaps in archival collections that sometimes perplex even seasoned sociohistorical investigators. Hence, prior to plunging into the practical nuts and bolts of archival research, I strongly encourage you to reflect on the broad sedimentary processes via which materials come to rest on archive shelves.

New researchers soon discover that any given person's or organization's archival papers may be housed in several different archives or be distributed (seemingly with little rationale) across a number of different collections in a single archive. This fragmentation is especially frustrating when, after completing a careful reading of a collection of papers on the last day of your visit to a distant repository, you discover (or the archivist casually mentions) several related collections that also bear directly, perhaps even more directly, on your inquiry. This is frustration incarnate: Why aren't these materials integrated and more systematically organized? The answer lies in the myriad routes and conditions under which materials are donated to archives. Borrowing from Alfred Schutz, I describe here the general deposition process as a series of *sedimentary* phases characterized by a multitude of erosions and reorderings.

The cumulative and reciprocal aspects of sedimentation in social processes were emphasized by Schutz (1970-1971, Vol. III) who observed that "the actual stock of knowledge is nothing but the *sedimentation* [emphasis added] of all our experiences of former definitions of previous situations" (p. 123). When researchers open a box of archival materials, the particular, concrete set of items in that box is the end product of an involved sedimentation process. The "sediment" in archives results directly from people defining certain materials—and not others—as "worth keeping" in archival situations. Conversely, it is from this accumulated sediment that researchers reconstruct and reinterpret our shared stock of knowledge in sociohistorical terms—and try to convince us that information about particular situations is "worth knowing." This is an endless and iterative loop, since what is worth knowing helps us, as a society, decide what is worth keeping, and so on and on.

Primary Sedimentation

The individuals and organizations whose papers are deposited in archives play important—and sometimes self-conscious—roles in helping determine what gets saved for posterity. This is the primary phase of archival sedimentation, in which people and organizations create, discard, save, collect, and donate materials of potential archival interest. For example, an active scholar's research, writing, and teaching over a lifetime of work generates a large mass of correspondence, manuscripts, lecture notes, and other materials. Academics also acquire a lot of other people's flotsam along the way: files of college memos, committee reports, books, publishers' catalogs, drafts of technical articles sent by colleagues, scholarly journals, unclaimed student papers, and so forth. All these materials are potential candidates for archival deposition, but whether, and in what condition, they will ever reach an archive has a lot to do with the scholar's definition of his or her own situation. What does the scholar think is worth keeping and for what purposes? Is the scholar careful or careless with papers he or she supposes should be saved? To explore some of these possibilities and their consequences, let's now follow the materials of a hypothetical scholar through this first and often unreflexive phase of archival sedimentation.

A HYPOTHETICAL EXAMPLE

Potential archival materials are neither created nor stored in abstract space; they are created and then repose over time at specific geographic places. The materials that may someday find a home in an archive accumulate over the years in a variety of places where our hypothetical scholar works and "sticks things away." These include, among other places, her university office in the anthropology building on a California campus, her laboratory space in the Anthropology Museum Annex, her California condominium, and a vacation cottage in Wisconsin (where she writes each summer). The way our scholar defines and maintains the mountains of materials that accumulate in all these places determines the universe of personal materials from which her future archival sediment, if any, will precipitate.

Our hypothetical scholar considers her accumulating letters, manuscripts, and so on to be "interesting," "useful someday," or just something to be "saved." For this reason, boxes of childhood mementos collect dust in the attic of her parents' home, and her office files bulge with all sorts of things. This is common behavior. Weinberg (1972), for example, wrote of sociologist Edward A. Ross: "Seemingly, Ross practiced what many of his generation felt to be a cardinal virtue: he saved and filed everything of any importance—report cards, manuscripts, typescripts, lecture appointments, financial records, copies of income tax statements, and newspaper clippings" (pp. 239-240).

If we assume our scholar is a pack rat like Ross, she still does not keep everything. Storage space is finite; there is never room for everything.

Our hypothetical academic succumbs to periodic urges to "clean house," resulting in the physical rearrangement of some materials and the discard of many others. Her potential archival deposit now erodes in unpredictable ways long before an archivist ever has a chance to evaluate what might be worth keeping. What she keeps and what she tosses has a direct bearing on what traces of her life's work future researchers may someday encounter in an archive. Our scholar keeps most of her correspondence, but she tosses out literally hundreds of letters from publishers and journal editors who rejected the manuscripts of her now well-known anthropological books and articles—she no longer wants to be reminded of those early rejections. On the other hand, our scholar is amused by her elementary school report cards—and keeps them. Some academics routinely keep very few mementos or personal papers, proudly cultivating the streamlined Protestant aesthetics of a clean desk and an uncluttered file cabinet. Erosion can also be accidental.

MORE FORMS OF EROSION

Erosion can take a serious toll even when individuals and organizations purposefully try to retain materials intended for archival preservation. Flood, fire, and other mishaps can wreck havoc upon paper records. For example, Roscoe Pound, the Dean of the Harvard Law School, lost, while moving from one city to another, much of the correspondence pertaining to his early professional career.[1] A large number of files belonging to the American Sociological Association were subjected to disarray and possible loss following a trucking accident during the ASA's move from New York City to new quarters in Washington, D.C.[2] Sociologist and journalist Ida B. Wells-Barnett lost a lifetime of irreplaceable newspaper articles when fires consumed her home.[3] Most of the correspondence, lecture notes, and books of an acquaintance of mine were ruined when a vindictive former spouse "stored" my friend's all too vulnerable materials in a ramshackle chicken coop exposed to the elements.[4] Most academics and many organizations, however, give little thought to archival preservation or the threat of flood, fire, and accident. Like our hypothetical scholar, they retain materials that they sense vaguely "might be useful someday," and that is as far as their archival consciousness develops.

Most people keep things, but we usually have no assurance that they save the most important or significant materials. For example, the term papers resting in our scholar's files may simply be those that indifferent students never bothered to pick up from her office. Hence, they do not represent her students' best work. If, as many people do, our scholar makes a habit of jotting quick replies to important letters on the letters themselves and thus sends the originals back to their senders, then the letters that gather dust in her file drawers may be precisely those she thought not worth answering. The really interesting memos may be the ones she crumpled in anger and threw into the wastebasket.

LOGIC-IN-USE

At issue is more than simply what our hypothetical scholar retains. There is also the manner in which she keeps it, a variation on the contrast between content and method. What is the method of our scholar's pack rat habits? Where does she keep things, and in what order? These questions are crucial because they influence the physical order and the completeness of the materials that eventually rest on archive shelves. Unless she simply piles one thing endlessly on top of another, creating a chronologically structured modern-day midden, she adds other, nonchronological complexities to her accumulation. Her "personal filing system" may be such that only she understands its rationale. Many academics of my acquaintance mix systematic filing with idiosyncratic practices having no apparent system.

Our scholar's logic-in-use for using, filing, rearranging, and storing materials affects the internal order of her accumulating materials. Sharply varied materials that are closely related in our scholar's mind (eclectic mementos from a trip abroad, for example) are thrown together in a drawer with no discernable rhyme or reason. At times, our scholar sifts through her files looking for items related to new topics of interest, removes a few items from their previous locations, and then refiles her selections together in new files, destroying the order in which she had for years arranged her materials while writing her first and still most influential book. The conceptual links that might have been suggested to us as researchers, had we been able to analyze the original arrangements and juxtapositions of her materials, will now be more difficult to discern through archival research.

Our scholar keeps the interrelated parts of her unfinished major project, which she intends to be her magnum opus, in four different places (her condominium, her laboratory, her office, and her vacation cottage, for example). This disjointed spatial reality will have consequences if she dies unexpectedly (as she now does, for purely didactic reasons, of course!). The odds are very low that all four parts of her project will be recovered, sent to the same archive, identified correctly, and filed appropriately together in the same storage box. It will help matters if she carefully labels all four parts of the project so that third parties will know what the materials are and how they relate to each other, but our scholar was engrossed in her project—she had no time and little personal rationale for attaching the detailed labels or memos that would help a third party piece the parts of the project together. She did not anticipate her untimely but didactically convenient death.

ARCHIVAL CONSEQUENCES

In an ideal typical scenario that reflects real life experiences in such cases, consider now the possible consequences of our scholar's spatially separated work habits. First, that part of the project left in our scholar's office is donated by her heirs—at the prodding of the university archivist —to the university archive in the campus library. Second, the part left on her laboratory table is quietly purloined by an ambitious young staff member at the university museum—wherein it reposes in his files for 35 years more and after which is donated together with his own papers to the university archive (where it remains today, its authorship unrecognized and never attributed to our hypothetical scholar). The third part, found in our scholar's condominium by her admiring stepson, is kept for 10 years as a memento but is finally donated to Harvard University (the stepson's alma mater), where it is placed in the anthropology archives of the Peabody Museum. The fourth and most central part of the project is a long and complex theory section on which our scholar spent many summers working. It now is swept into the dust bin when a commercial cleaning crew is hired by her legal executor to clean up the Wisconsin cottage so it can be sold expeditiously to settle our late scholar's estate. Through such scenarios in real life, of which the variations are nearly endless, the papers of active intellectuals are lost, fragmented, and dispersed.

A few academics are keenly aware of the potential archival value of their papers and correspondence and take pains to preserve them. They might officially appoint a literary executor in their will (a prudent step in any case), or work with an archive to make preposthumous arrangements for the preservation of their papers. Indeed, you do not have to be dead to donate your papers to an archive that will have them. The late Chicago sociologist Morris Janowitz, for example, donated the bulk of his papers to the University of Chicago and, before his death, assisted in their labeling and archival arrangement.[5] In practice, however, many—perhaps most—social scientists, their colleagues, and their families wrongly discount the archival utility of scholarly papers, giving no thought to their safekeeping. If the papers of such scholars do somehow make it to an archive, the resulting archival sediment is likely to be partial, fragmented, and uneven.

When individuals die, the first broad phase of archival sedimentation comes definitely to a close. The deceased write no more, discard nothing more, nor ever again tamper with the structural order of their papers and files. A new phase of sedimentation begins in which other people, third parties, do as they will with the surviving physical traces that sociohistorical investigators like yourself might someday like to analyze.

Secondary Sedimentation

During the second phase of archival sedimentation, the order and condition in which individuals leave their papers and personal effects at the time of death becomes crucially important. Unless preempted by careful planning and/or the appointment of an energetic and capable literary executor, this second phase has no sure outcome. The situation is uncertain and liminal (Turner, 1969; Deegan, 1989; Deegan & Hill, 1991a). A deceased writer's papers go up for grabs, suspended betwixt and between oblivion and preservation.

The uncertainty of this phase is increased by the wide range of potential motives and abilities of the people who now evaluate, discard, and/or preserve the personal papers of the deceased before they are transmitted, if ever, to a formal archive. Opportunities for erosion multiply. A vindictive department head tries to obliterate the memory of a despised rival by destroying the deceased's office files; a family member discovers and burns the deceased's torrid love letters on the assumption that the deceased's personal life is no one else's business; an overly devoted literary executor, attempting to preserve the deceased's professional reputation unblemished, finds and destroys a cache of letters in which the deceased was once charged with plagiarism, and so on. The point is that any number of people with a wide variety of motives make consequential decisions about what to do with the deceased's papers.

A scholarly life is by definition one of social interaction with students, colleagues, critics, and mentors. Active scholars not only create and keep mountains of materials (the focus of this discussion so far), they also send and give large amounts of original materials to others. They write letters to friends, send manuscripts to publishers for review, write comments on students' exams, distribute copies of unpublished papers at professional meetings, and so on. An important aspect of secondary sedimentation concerns what all the people to whom materials are sent during a scholar's lifetime do with those materials. Do they keep them or discard them?

Secondary sedimentation, with reference to our hypothetical scholar per se, is simultaneously primary sedimentation when viewed in terms of the accumulation habits of our scholar's friends, students, and colleagues. Thus, because the interaction network of friends, students, and colleagues is potentially so very large, the complexity of archival sedimentation explodes exponentially. This situation has potentially negative and positive consequences. Negatively, it means that traces of our scholar's intellectual life might come to rest in any number of archives (not to mention other places), and that tracking them all down may be a difficult, expensive, and time-consuming task. Positively, if a writer's interpersonal network is dense and complex, it increases the overall probability that archival traces can be found somewhere if investigators are patient and diligent searchers.

The importance and possibility of sedimentations in other people's files should never be disregarded by sociohistorical investigators. Such deposits may be the only places in which traces of a person in whom you are interested may have survived. For example, the 19th-century social scientist and political economist, Harriet Martineau, implored all of her correspondents to burn the letters she wrote during her lifetime. Many took this command seriously and literally. Others, however, sometimes in a deep moral quandary, valued the letters as much too important to destroy and kept them among their own personal effects. Much that we know about Martineau today is due to those surviving letters—letters that Martineau would have destroyed if given the chance.

The foundational book in symbolic interactionism (if not social psychology as a whole) is George Herbert Mead's (1934) *Mind, Self & Society*. It provides another, instructive example. *Mind, Self & Society* is available today only because of sedimentations in other people's files. Mead's seminal book was published after his death by Charles W. Morris, an editor who pieced the book together from classroom notes taken and saved by Mead's former students at the University of Chicago.[6] Mead's own lecture notes did not survive, but the notes of his students, who thought them too valuable to throw away, did endure—and many of Mead's ideas with them.

Letters, memos, official documents, and the like accumulate in many disparate places beyond the grasp of the individual writers and scholars who create such materials. A few locations include: department, college, and university files; the personal accumulations of colleagues and former students; publishing houses; journal editors' offices; the files of professional organizations to which the scholars belonged and/or held office; the private collections of admiring "fans"; and, of course, the ubiquitous attics and basements of personal friends. Materials in these many locations can easily escape the best intentions of a literary executor or an intrepid researcher. At the same time, their very profusion increases the odds that we will find something useful if we are diligent and resourceful. As archival investigators, we must be always alert to the myriad locations in which secondary sedimentations might unexpectedly settle.

Tertiary Sedimentation

Tertiary sedimentation refers to the sorting, erosion, and arrangement of materials after arrival at an archive. Such materials may flow directly from the person who created them, but more commonly they arrive via secondary mediation. Third parties decide directly that all or part of an individual's papers should be saved and donate them to an archive. Alternatively, materials are preserved indirectly via the accumulations and subsequent archival deposits of people with whom the scholar interacted. In a few cases, materials are donated by private collectors, and in still other situations, finances permitting, archivists may aggressively collect certain types of manuscripts and rare books. When an individual's papers, manuscripts, books, and miscellaneous memorabilia arrive at an archive for deposition, they come into the province of archival curators.

There is no guarantee, however, that an archive will accept all or even part of any given donation. Archival space and finances are limited. An archivist may judge that, although it would be nice to accept every relevant donation, the available resources are insufficient to properly organize and maintain all materials as archival collections. A corollary is that donors sometimes have to shop around for an archive that will accept a particular donation, with the result that some deposits wind up in rather unexpected places.[7] Curators typically accept donations contingent on having discretion to discard (or return to the donors) materials they deem unimportant or not appropriate to the mission of their archive. But what may be of no significance to a given archivist might be crucial to socio-historical researchers, depending on the questions they want to answer! Thus, a third sedimentary phase unfolds in which archivists accept or reject materials according to their own interests and the priorities of the organizations for which they work. Archivists also sort, organize, and inventory materials in preparation for public use.

The archivists who yearly sort through countless boxes of donated papers often know little about the people who collected or created the materials therein. It is a curator's task, however, to "make sense of" what can be literally thousands of letters and mountains of other matter in any given donation. The materials must be evaluated and given at least a preliminary storage site. It may be years, however, before a deposit is thoroughly prepared, indexed, and described in a detailed finding aid (Chapter 6). Indeed, formal preparation may be indefinitely postponed while other, "more important" donations leap ahead in the processing queue.

THE ARCHIVIST'S PRIORITIES

The priorities that archivists use to accept and process donations, and the schemes that archivists use to organize and index specific collections, are the central features of tertiary sedimentation. Archival priorities and organizational practices directly influence what materials researchers find in archives and the condition in which they find them. Like publishers who publish books they judge will sell, archivists tend to accept collections they think sociohistorical researchers will actually use for research. Archivists gladly accept the papers of distinguished and well-known individuals, as such collections usually lend prestige to archives—and to the archivists who successfully encourage such donations.

In this way, archives mirror the societies in which they are embedded. The papers of privileged and institutionally powerful people are far more likely to be accepted by archives than are donations of "lesser" men and women. A few archives do try to obtain representative materials that reflect the lives of ordinary people, but even these archives cannot hope to build comprehensive collections for every individual who might like to donate his or her papers and memorabilia. There are too many people and far too little archival space to go around.

It is not an abstract exercise when archivists favor donations they think investigators will actually use. They have in mind the flesh-and-blood people who come to archives year after year to consult archival collections. Those researchers hail typically from the humanities, not the social sciences, with the result that the content of archival collections is often biased away from the typical research interests of, for example, sociologists or economists. All things equal, archives more readily accept the papers of poets, novelists, and historians than those of professionals in other disciplines. Nonetheless, the papers of many social scientists can be found in archives, typically in those maintained by colleges and universities, simply because academic organizations are willing to accept the papers of their own faculty members and those of particularly successful alumni. The interests of the organization that sponsors and pays for an archive play a consequential role in determining what gets saved in archives. In some cases, archives are little more than depositories for official organizational records that bureaucrats use in the course of an organization's day-to-day business. The point is that archivists' preferences and prejudices, combined with organizational goals and directives, work toward the archival preservation of certain kinds of materials rather than others during tertiary sedimentation.

THE ARCHIVIST'S SENSE OF ORDER

When an individual's papers arrive at an archive for deposition, the materials are frequently in disarray (think of the state of your own desk drawers, or the boxes of "stuff" in your attic or basement!). Archivists must sort through the material and arrange it for public use. Each donation is usually designated as a "collection" identified by the name of the person who wrote or collected the bulk of the papers in the donation. Typically, within a collection, curators group like materials with like, that is, letters with letters, lecture notes with lecture notes, book manuscripts with book manuscripts, scrapbooks with scrapbooks, and so forth. Within these broad categories, or series, however, materials are typically arranged chronologically. The prevalence of chronological schemes in part reflects the kinds of questions that historians and other humanists have traditionally asked when using archival materials. The way in which materials in collections are organized by archivists is consequential for the researchers who use archives, as we shall see in subsequent chapters.

In brief, archivists typically arrange correspondence by date rather than by subject matter or correspondent. Thus, for example, an archival box might contain a writer's letters from 1939 in 12 folders, one folder for each month of the year. Within each folder, letters are usually arranged sequentially by day of the month. Thus, a writer's personal filing system is often obliterated. For example, a group of letters from a friend that an individual kept in a special file are now separated, interfiled chronologically with dentist's bills, manuscript reviews, travel authorizations, and birthday cards. Once archivists impose a new, chronological order, they intend that their chronologies be maintained.

There are, of course, any number of possible exceptions to the general chronological scheme. For example, a subsequent, large donation of additional letters by the same writer for the same year might be appended to the collection in an *addendum*, leaving the initial archival arrangement undisturbed. Some writers put carbon copies of their outgoing letters in bound "letter books," and curators typically keep these intact—often in a separate series within a collection. In many collections, outgoing and incoming letters are interfiled; in others they are maintained in separate chronological series.

Nonmanuscript items in a donation are sometimes severed from the main collection and separately arranged. Family photographs are often sent to photograph collections in a different department within the archive. So, too, paintings, sound recordings, videotapes, motion pictures, and so on may be assigned separate locations. If a scholar's library is preserved intact, the volumes are likely rearranged, perhaps by author, and not grouped on shelves as the scholar would have done herself. When the formal processing of new collections is finally complete, the materials may indeed rest in archival configurations that would be foreign or puzzling to the people who originally created or kept them.

Thus, through the processes of primary, secondary, and tertiary sedimentation, materials come to rest in boxes and file folders, on shelves and in vaults behind the locked doors of archival repositories. These materials are archival sediment, residual traces of human activity. They are selective traces, however, filtered by the combined imprint of personal machinations and idiosyncrasies, family sensibilities, professional envy and collegial admiration, organizational mandates, bureaucratic decisions, archival traditions, social structure, power, wealth, and institutional inertia. From such traces, we seek data from which to make sense of individuals, organizations, social movements, and sociohistorical settings.

NOTES

1. Letter, Pound to Sayre, 31 October 1948, Paul Sayre Collection, University of Iowa Archives, Iowa City, Iowa.

2. Letter, Gresham M. Sykes to Aero Mayflower Transit Company, 16 October 1963, Papers of the American Sociological Association, Manuscript Division, Library of Congress, Washington, DC.

3. Finding aid to the Ida B. Wells-Barnett Papers, Special Collections, Joseph Regenstein Library, University of Chicago, Chicago, IL. Wells-Barnett published numerous articles in Afro-American newspapers that were neither microfilmed nor in libraries.

4. Personal communication.

5. In such situations, donors usually place restrictions on who may examine the collection while the donor is still alive. Thus, in the case at hand, one needed to obtain Mr. Janowitz's written permission before access could be granted by the University of Chicago archivist.

6. For the details of this case, see Morris's editorial preface in Mead (1934, v-vii).

7. The deposition of Russian social scientist and Harvard sociologist Pitirim Sorokin's papers in a Canadian archive in Saskatchewan illustrates just how far afield a scholar's papers can go.

3. STRUCTURE, CONTROL, AND TECHNOLOGY

The structural characteristics of archives set them sharply apart from most libraries even though archival repositories usually share superficial resemblances to the latter. It behooves novice investigators having experience only with library research to prepare mentally for a radically new set of protocols. You must learn to work productively within a very different set of structural constraints. The cold reality, which is taken lightly only at your peril, is that archival curators wield considerable power over the materials in their charge. The major structural issues include: (a) access to materials, (b) the uniqueness of archival materials, (c) the noncirculation of materials, (d) property rights, and (e) the "closed stacks" organization of archival repositories. Recent developments in computer, microform, and photocopy technologies, however, pose interesting questions concerning the future import of these structural issues.

Access to Archives

Physical access to archival repositories is restricted, sometimes very tightly. Gaining physical entry to an archive is an obvious but fundamentally necessary prerequisite for serious and sustained archival research. Permission to enter an archive is either prearranged and later confirmed upon arrival, or is granted outright during the orientation interview (Chapter 5). Curators, who are rightly concerned about theft, vandalism, and needless wear and tear on irreplaceable materials, can—and sometimes do —deny entry. The crucial point is that access to archival repositories is not guaranteed.

By contrast, entry to libraries may not be automatic, but the consequences are usually less severe. A few university research libraries, for example, limit entrance to their own faculty, students, and alumni. It is unlikely, however, that any given library has the only copy of a particular book. If permission to use a specific library is denied, you can go to comparable libraries to find other copies of the books you want. Even rare or obscure books can usually be obtained, if only in microform versions, via interlibrary loans.

If entry to an archive is denied, by contrast, your proposed project may be seriously injured and perhaps ended. There is likely no alternative archive having identical materials. Happily, because academics and advanced graduate students already possess demonstrable institutional legitimation, most readers of this book will gain archival entry with relative ease. Undergraduate students, independent scholars, and persons with tenuous institutional affiliations, however, may have more difficulty and should arrange for letters of introduction prior to archival visits.[1] Students may be asked to produce a letter from a sponsoring faculty member.

The range of strictures varies widely. In small archives, entry often depends on the mood, whim, and schedule of the appointed curator. In larger archives, bureaucratic entrance requirements are more formal and are rigidly enforced. Archives maintained by public and some semipublic entities are typically less restrictive and are essentially open to the public. Admission to local historical society archives sometimes requires nothing more than signing a guest register. Applicants to archives should, however, always be prepared to produce at least one photo ID, such as a driver's license, current student identification card, or a valid passport. It is prudent to contact an archive beforehand to determine how best to meet the archive's entrance requirements.

Gaining admission is sometimes only the first step. Archival materials are usually grouped together in any number of collections within an archive. The next task may be to gain permission to use materials in particular collections. In some highly restrictive archives, access to each collection must be separately negotiated, typically during the orientation interview or in subsequent interviews. Even in relatively open archives, a few collections may be restricted to certain categories of users and/or require advance written permission from a literary executor or the donors of the material. Access to an archive does not necessarily entail access to every collection within the archive. Hence, it behooves you to determine in advance whether special permission must be obtained to use specific collections in which you are likely to be interested.

Uniqueness of Archival Materials

The reason archival access is so important is because archived materials are typically unique, irreplaceable, one-of-a-kind items that cannot be obtained elsewhere. Uniqueness is a structural reality of the world that makes access to specific archives essential for particular projects. A library per se is similar to an archive in this regard only when a library has the only known copies of particular books. The uniqueness of archival materials justifies archive entrance requirements and the strict enforcement of reading room protocols designed to protect irreplaceable materials.

Social scientists who study social trends based on census data, or conduct random digit telephone surveys, or engage in participant observer studies should think soberly about the research consequences of depending on unique materials. Irreplaceable data sources are foreign to the traditional logic of much social scientific research. If your computer crashes and you lose your census data, you simply order a backup tape. If randomly selected subjects in a survey refuse to answer, you simply replace them from a pool of alternate respondents. If we lose legitimacy in a participant observer setting, we can usually begin again in another locale because our interest is in generalizable social processes, not in a specific, irreplaceable setting per se. Sociohistorical research, however, often builds on unique data about specific people and organizations.

If, for example, you set out to discover the specific sociohistorical circumstances in which the likes of Jane Addams, W. E. B. DuBois, Charlotte Perkins Gilman, or Max Weber each developed their particular social scientific perspectives, then you must have access to certain repositories and archival collections. Substitutes will not suffice! Hence, it pays to take access issues seriously. Your requests for admission must be professional, well planned, and thoughtfully rationalized. If an archivist says "No, I'm sorry, but you cannot use the collection," you may have few viable alternatives (possible exceptions are discussed in Chapter 11).

Noncirculating Materials and Spatiotemporal Constraints

Archival materials are not only unique, they are almost always noncirculating; that is, they cannot be checked out or obtained through interlibrary loans. Because archival materials are unique, and because archives do not loan archival materials, researchers are necessarily obliged to travel to an archive and remain in its vicinity for as long as access to the archive's unique resources is required. A thorough search of any given archival deposit may take days, weeks, or even months. As a result, several unavoidable structural contingencies must be successfully mediated.

Unless relevant archival resources are available locally, certain spatiotemporal contingencies become crucial. These include the time and expense of travel to distant archives and for finding food and lodging. In addition, your work schedule must conform to the hours during which an archive is open, typically from 9:00 a.m. to 5:00 p.m., Monday through Friday, although a few archives provide extended hours and/or weekend access.[2] Many smaller archives close during the lunch hour and may be open only a few days per month. Most archives observe the standard holidays, and many university archives close during local festivities such as commencement exercises. These structural constraints tend to confine the use of archival materials to local scholars and to those fortunate others with sufficient time and money to make the required trip(s).[3]

As with many ostensibly available facilities in this society, archives are effectively open only to those who can afford to make use of them. It matters little if you garner a letter ensuring your access to restricted collections if you cannot take time from family, work, or school obligations—or pay travel costs—to make effective use of your entrée. The financial and spatiotemporal realities of this situation illustrate how access to data—and thus to knowledge—is shaped by the allocation of wealth, income, and other resources. Your decision to pursue an archival research project should include a realistic appraisal of the financial and spatiotemporal constraints under which your anticipated work will be conducted.

Property Rights

Unlike benefactors who make gifts of books to libraries,[4] the donors of archival materials (as well as their heirs and/or literary executors) frequently retain private property rights over materials deposited in archives. In some cases, donors permit materials to be used only by scholars who receive the approval of the donor (or of the executor or heirs). Donors sometimes place stranglehold restrictions on the quotation, copying, and publication of materials they donate to archives (see also Chapter 10). Archives sometimes agree to these stipulations to entice the donation of particularly desirable collections.

Letters, unpublished articles, and other manuscript material in archives are intellectual properties protected by copyright laws (Strong, 1990). Copyright for a letter resides in most cases with the person who wrote it, not with the person to whom it was sent or addressed. In some cases, copyrights are signed over to an archive when a donation is made. In others, the donor (or the donor's heirs or executor) retains his or her intellectual property rights, but this can lead to unexpectedly complex situations. For example, permission from a donor to read and publish letters in a restricted collection by no means conveys permission to publish letters in the collection that were written by persons other than the donor. The point here is that access to and dissemination of information in archives are often subject to proprietary controls.

Closed Stacks

Archival materials are usually stored in restricted areas or closed stacks to which patrons are almost always denied physical access. Researchers must request or "page" materials for use, and this provides a mechanism by which archivists monitor the nature and quantity of materials consulted by researchers. Upon request, materials are retrieved from the stacks and brought to the reading room where researchers may study them. As a result, archives have the structural properties of what Goffman (1959) called front and backstage regions. Structurally, researchers have no way to verify what materials are actually in the stacks or whether their use of materials is hindered by unseen obfuscation.

The opportunity for deception is an irreducible structural fact of life in all social scientific investigation (Goffman, 1974), including archival research. In the present case, if patrons are told that certain materials have been misplaced or taken out of circulation for repair and restoration, patrons have no way to personally check the veracity of these statements. The structural arrangement of archives provides archivists with a mechanism to deny access to materials backstage even while appearing publicly helpful and open in the reading room or front region. How often this structural situation is exploited to control and limit access to materials cannot

—by its very nature—be verified. Documentation by Goffman (1974) and Bok (1978) of rampant fabrication by professionals in modern life weighs heavily toward the hypothesis that archivists sometimes control their patrons by untruthfully reporting that requested materials cannot be found. Structurally speaking, it is very easy for an archivist to make life difficult for a troublesome or irritating patron. If for no other reason, researchers should strive to maintain cordial, friendly, and professional relations with archivists and their staff.

Technology and Control

Ongoing technological developments are shifting the nature of structural control in archives. Three developments are especially important: personal computers, microforms, and photocopy machines. Computer technology is currently the least developed and least applied innovation in archival research. Expanding networks of on-line archival indexes, however, facilitate searches for potentially relevant collections and may eventually allow detailed searches of archival indexes (Chapter 6) prior to on-site visits. Several archives now allow the use of laptop or notebook computers for note taking, and archives may soon permit patrons to scan archival documents directly into computer imaging and word processing files.

Microform technologies are well developed, but only a relatively few archival collections are available on microfilm. Even with aggressive microfilming programs, the high temporal and financial costs of filming even a moderately sized collection leave the vast majority of an archive's material unfilmed. Microfilm allows new freedoms, however, including interlibrary loans and sales to libraries. These freedoms reduce archival hegemony and ameliorate spatiotemporal constraints. But film copies also generate a new category of special privilege in which archivists permit further access to the original documents only under very special circumstances. To date, the application of microform technology alters but little the necessity for travel to distant archives. With a few notable exceptions, such as the papers of Jane Addams, W. E. B. DuBois, Harriet Martineau, or Edward A. Ross, the papers of most social scientists are, at present, unlikely candidates for microfilming.

Of the major new technologies to impact archival research, photocopying is presently the most beneficial to researchers. It permits shorter archival visits (visits now devoted largely to tagging items for photocopying rather than to study of documents in the archive per se). Photocopying reduces errors introduced through note taking. Photocopy enlargements and contrast control can retrieve faint or fading images from original documents. Compared to the cost of filming an entire collection, photocopies are produced inexpensively "on demand" at the request of researchers. Investment in photocopies secures a relevant set of archival documents with which to later work at one's leisure.[5] Archives vary considerably, however, as to procedures for requesting and making photocopies and in the amount of photocopying permitted.[6]

Structural constraints on archival research have been ameliorated in recent years by advances in technological development, but only modestly so. Overall access to needed archival deposits remains firmly under the supervision and control of professional archivists. It is difficult to overestimate the central role of archivists and their structural prerogatives in the success or failure of archivally based sociohistorical research projects. The first steps to archival success, however, typically start long before making a trip to a repository. Veteran investigators avoid a lot of frustration by first developing and implementing preliminary archival search strategies appropriate to their research questions.

NOTES

1. If required, letters of introduction from recognized scholars in your field of inquiry, the administrator of a local historical society, or faculty members at a local college or university should do the trick. Such letters should attest to your valid need to use the archive in question and request all possible assistance from the archive in helping you achieve your research goals.

2. When available, access during evening hours or weekends often depends on having made formal application for admission during the archive's regular weekday business hours.

3. Many scholars on limited budgets combine archiving trips with other travel when possible, including travel to professional meetings, vacations, and so forth. Small travel grants are available to students and faculty at many colleges. Graduate students should check specifically for dissertation travel grants. The National Endowment for the Humanities currently provides small grants to academics and independent scholars for travel to archives. Check with your university's grants and contracts office for additional funding sources.

4. Donors of personal library collections are sometimes able to stipulate that the collections will be maintained *ensemble* or under lock and key, but librarians tend to resist such stipulations and sometimes ignore them after the donor's death.

5. Charges for photocopies typically range from 10 to 25 cents per page, and in one instance as much as $1.00 per copy. Thus, individual photocopies are inexpensive, but copying hundreds of pages can be costly.

6. Some archives permit self-service copying, but permission to copy must still be obtained from the archivist. Some archives limit researchers to as few as 50 copies total, while others impose virtually no limit.

4. GETTING STARTED:"TARGETS" AND "TOOL KITS"

This chapter outlines the systematic preparations that are fundamental to efficient, productive searches for archival deposits. The focal point of this groundwork is a constant emphasis on the importance of names in archival organization and discovery. A primary, name-oriented search strategy is advanced here, supplemented by two alternative approaches (topical searches and local searches) for starting archival projects. Systematic preliminaries include: (a) selecting and naming a search "target" and (b) compiling three sets of auxiliary "tool kits": review bibliographies, master biography files, and master name lists. Taken together, the contents of these tool kits significantly increase your odds of locating potentially useful archival deposits.

Names and Archival Research: Naming a Target

When archivists ask, "What specifically are you looking for?" during orientation interviews (Chapter 5), they expect you to present a list of names in reply. The proper names of people and organizations are guiding elements in the social construction of most archival collections. This situation derives from the historian's traditional interest in specific individuals and their accomplishments. Sociobiographical projects, in particular, are thus well suited to name-oriented searches for archival materials. There are many prominent social scientists, government agencies, professional societies, academic organizations, and formal associations for whom the name-oriented strategy is especially appropriate. Even if your research program is fundamentally topical rather than biographical, note carefully that archival practice is heavily biased in favor of your knowing specific names of persons and/or organizations associated with your topical theme.

For example, assume you plan to document the collective professional history of criminologists, nurses, or social workers. To quickly locate useful repositories, you would need a list of specific people and organizations associated with the origins and subsequent development of the professional group you choose to study. Similarly, if your interest is in labor movements, progressive politics, or social change during the Great Depression, you need to know the names of specific people and organizations directly involved in those sociohistorical phenomena. The operational point is this: It is in concrete documents—linked by names through archival directories, finding aids, and archival indexes to specific archival collections—that you will discover archived data for sociohistorical analysis.

The premise here is that you have already identified and chosen (or your instructor has assigned!) a named target (e.g., a specific person, organization, or social movement) to study archivally.[1] The target you select focuses the compilation of your archival tool kits and guides your search for repositories. Keep in mind, however, that it is not unusual to shift focus as a project unfolds, thus expanding the search process to any number of new targets. For the sake of clarity, the following discussion assumes a single archival target. Knowing the proper name of your target and learning the proper names of individuals and organizations associated with your target is the key to building your tool kits and identifying archives that you should visit. The process for learning this matrix of names begins with bibliographical and biographical work in your local library.

Compiling Archival Tool Kits

Having identified a named target as a focus, you are ready to compile three archival tool kits that will stand in ready service throughout your archival project. The contents of each tool kit typically expand throughout the life of a project and serve a variety of purposes. The *master name list*, however, is crucial to the name-oriented search strategy for locating archival collections. In turn, the master name list derives from your compilation of the *master bibliography* and a *master biography file*.

MASTER BIBLIOGRAPHY

The first step in archival research is a standard literature review.[2] Check the *National Union Catalog* and *Dissertation Abstracts International* for major published studies about your target.[3] Relevant periodical indexes and abstracts should also be searched for authoritative articles.[4] Record the bibliographic information for each relevant reference on index cards or in a computer file. This file is your master bibliography. It will be invaluable when you draft the final bibliography for your paper, dissertation, or book. In the meantime, your master bibliography leads you to publications that (a) help direct and shape your research project, (b) provide historical data for your master biography file, and (c) equip you with ready-made lists of names for your master name list.

It is useful to know what other researchers have already discovered, if anything, about your archival target. Discovering a good published study about your target often saves a lot of groundwork. In fact, after reviewing the major studies listed in your master bibliography, you may decide that the archival work you planned to undertake has already been covered satisfactorily by other scholars. On the other hand, the published literature is more likely to suggest holes to plug, new questions to answer, or old puzzles to reexamine. A literature review should also produce many basic facts for your master biography file (discussed in next section). In addition, the footnotes, acknowledgments, and bibliographies in scholarly publications often identify rich, pertinent archival deposits and may refer you to obscure published works you might have missed in your literature search.

Pragmatically, the name index in a germane scholarly monograph often provides a core list of people and organizations associated with your target. These names should be identified and entered in your master name list (discussed later in this chapter). Unless the monograph was written by an astute social scientist, however, it is unlikely that it provides a comprehensive list of your target's professional, organizational, and intellectual contacts in the social sciences.

If you plan to write your target's intellectual biography, this is a good time to assemble a comprehensive bibliography of your target's published works. It may be pointless to continue such a project if you cannot identify a significant body of work written by your target. Note that scholarly monographs about social scientists often contain detailed bibliographies of a target's works, but the entries may be "selected" and should therefore be verified for accuracy and inclusiveness. A conventional bibliographic search should be executed "from scratch" to locate as many of your target's works as possible. Scan the standard sources, including the *National Union Catalog, Social Sciences Citation Index, Sociological Abstracts*, and other disciplinary-specific abstracts.[5]

Relatively recent bibliographic aids, however, like *Sociological Abstracts* (begun in 1952) and *Social Sciences Citation Index* (begun in 1972), are inadequate for locating journal articles written by early social scientists. If you are hunting for works written during the founding eras of the social science disciplines, turn first to aids like the *Combined Retrospective*

Index Set to Journals in Sociology, 1895-1974; the *Combined Retrospective Index Set to Journals in History, 1838-1974*; and the *Combined Retrospective Index to Journals in Political Science, 1886-1974*, but use caution. For example, the 1895-1935 index to the *American Journal of Sociology* lists seven items written by former American Sociological Society president George Elliott Howard, but five of the seven are not listed in the *Combined Retrospective Index Set to Journals in Sociology*. To conduct a comprehensive search, inspect firsthand all journals in which your target may have published.[6] For early essays published in less specialized journals, consult the *Cumulative Author Index for Poole's Index to Periodical Literature, 1802-1906*; the *Nineteenth Century Readers' Guide to Periodical Literature, 1890-1899*; and the early volumes of the *International Index to Periodicals* (now the *Social Science Index*). You stand a good chance of locating the contemporary critical reception of your target's published works in the *Combined Retrospective Index to Book Reviews in Scholarly Journals, 1886-1974*.[7] Add the names of your target's reviewers to your master name list.

MASTER BIOGRAPHY FILE

Your master biography file is a "who's who"-style data bank on the target of your archival investigation. As you proceed further in your study, you will add information on other key figures. During the "getting started" stage, however, keep the compilation of your master biography file focused sharply on your initial target. You can immediately construct a provisional summary sketch of your target's career based on your file and, more importantly, your master biography file is the direct input for generating the all-important master name list.

If your target is a person who made almost any kind of a mark in the world, you will be able to find out something about his or her career by using an array of biographical dictionaries, encyclopedias, and other compilations, to which *BioBase*[8] and the *Biography and Genealogy Master Index* are excellent indexes. These specialized reference sources are available in most research libraries. An especially helpful biographical source is the *National Cyclopædia of American Biography*.[9] Other valuable sources include the *Dictionary of American Biography*; *Who Was Who in America*; *Notable American Women*; *American Women Writers*; *American Men and Women of Science—The Social and Behavioral Sciences*; *International Encyclopedia of the Social Sciences*; *Contemporary Authors*; and the forthcoming *American National Biography*. Local "who's who" compilations that might escape inclusion in *BioBase* should also be consulted, as should obituary notices in professional journals and relevant local newspapers. For persons of national stature, the *New York Times Index* points to useful obituaries. State and local historical societies may offer indexes to obituaries in local newspapers.

If your named target is a formal organization, social movement, or some other social phenomenon, a variety of historical reference aids should be checked now if they were not canvassed during your literature search. Useful titles include: *Historical Abstracts*; *America: History and Life*; and the *Combined Retrospective Index to Journals in History, 1838-1974*. Consult Sheehy (1986) and confer with your reference librarian about additional historical and biographical aids, especially if your target was a foreign national or non-U.S. social phenomenon.

Collect the biographical accounts you discover in a special file folder marked "Master Biography File" and take them with you on archiving trips. Most entries in the biographical aids listed above are brief, from a single paragraph to, at most, a few pages. Do not let the brevity fool you, because even very short entries, such as those in *Who Was Who in America*, often add a new and useful nugget of information. Make photocopies of each entry (and, as you may want to cite them later, be sure to jot down complete bibliographic references).

The preliminary biographical information you have collected, together with any information gathered during your literature review, enables you, if you so elect, to write a summary sketch of your target's career. Life history sketches can, of course, be written for organizations, social movements, and individuals alike. Your provisional sketch briefly outlines what you know about your target up to this point. Such sketches are often integral elements in grant applications and dissertation proposals. To orient archivists to the identity, life, and accomplishments of your target, you can enclose a copy of your sketch when you write to archivists about the potential relevance of various collections for your project.

It is not mandatory that you compose a biographical sketch of your target, but many researchers find that doing so helps orient their subsequent work. Composing a concise sketch forces you to identify life situations and events that you consider important, and gives you an early opportunity to recognize lacunae in your understanding of your target. Deegan's (1988b) primer on locating biographical data about women sociologists and the essays in Deegan's (1991) *Women in Sociology* and

Gacs, Khan, McIntyre, and Weinberg's (1988) *Women Anthropologists* are excellent exemplars of what one can accomplish, and the kinds of sketches you can write, based on library research using *BioBase* and published sources.[10]

MASTER NAME LIST

The master name list is the key to locating archival deposits in a name-oriented archival search strategy. Your name list is, in a sense, the cast of characters in an unfolding archival drama. A comprehensive list includes understudies as well as principal actors. You will add many new players to the list as your archival work progresses. Some names will play surprisingly minor roles; others will give unexpectedly rich performances. Your list will have several uses, but its first purpose is to help you search for relevant archives. Keep your name list on index cards, one name to a card, or in an alphabetically arranged computer file.

To compile your list, scan the biographical data you have collected and list all the proper names you find.[11] List the names of individuals who obviously knew your target, such as family members, friends, and professional colleagues. Look for names of parents, siblings, spouses, children, in-laws, and famous relatives; list names of mentors, close friends, and known professional associates. Next, collect the names of businesses, agencies, and political, social, and professional organizations in which the target worked, volunteered, held membership, participated, or simply frequented. Note the names of communities in which your target lived and worked; gather names, dates, and locations of schools attended. Note, too, that writers who have published scholarly studies or biographies about your target may have archival deposits of their own that contain unused, unpublished materials that will be valuable to your study.[12] Add the names of major biographers to your master name list.

Identify your target comprehensively in terms of alternate names by which he or she was known (i.e., birth name, married names, pseudonyms, legal name changes, etc.). Note also that organizations sometimes change their names. For example, the American Sociological Association (ASA) was formerly the American Sociological Society (ASS). Pay particular attention to changes in the married names of female targets,[13] but male names can also be problematic. For example, the well-known jurist Roscoe Pound was born Nathan Roscoe Pound. Although he never used *Nathan* as an adult, Pound's archival papers at the Nebraska State Historical Society are nonetheless filed under his birth name. Idiosyncrasy no doubt plays a part in such matters. For example, when checking the full names that male faculty members used on their doctoral dissertations, I found recently that 8 of 12 men in one social science department now use significantly altered names. Immigrants who Americanize their names provide another common source of naming complexity.

When your target is a named organization or social movement, assemble a provisional list of leaders and other participants, and collect the names of other groups, agencies, or associations having interorganizational ties, overlapping memberships, or shared objectives with your target organization.

Your master name list will have many handy uses throughout your research project. For example, variant spellings of a target's name may be the key that locates an otherwise hidden archival deposit or that later helps you correctly attribute early publications or organization memberships. Remember, too, that computerized searches require precise spelling, and the computer listing you want may be tucked away under a variant spelling, a maiden name, or a married woman's husband's name, for example.

During the orientation interview (Chapter 5), when the archivist asks, "What specifically are you looking for?" your name list helps you frame a knowledgeable reply. For example (substituting real names for the hypothetical letters), "I would like to see any collections related to the life and work of X; the family, friends, and colleagues of X, specifically A, H, S, and P; and the organizations in which X is known to have participated, specifically R and W."

When you later consult finding aids (Chapter 6) for specific archival collections, you will be able to assess more quickly whether a collection likely holds many or few documents related to people who knew your target. Your name list will also be helpful when you read archival documents. If, for example, you read a letter from "John" to "Mary" that discusses the recent illness of "cousin William," your name list and your biographical file will help you sort out "who's who" in such domestic dramas. Your task at this point, however, is to use your master name list to locate potentially useful archival repositories.

The Name-Oriented Search for Archival Collections

A major puzzle in archival research is how to find archives and collections useful to your investigation. There is no surefire solution to this problem, and success depends on a combination of system, persistence, and serendipity. This situation is compounded by the reality that one does not always know, in specific terms, where an archival project will ultimately lead. Armed with your master name list, however, locating the archives that most likely contain relevant materials is a straightforward task.

Ideally, your initial target donated personal and professional papers to a major archive where they were accepted and carefully processed for research use. To locate such deposits, look under your target's name in the *National Union Catalog of Manuscript Collections*.[14] This major source is published in several volumes, with supplements, by the Library of Congress and is available in most research libraries. Using the *Catalog* is greatly facilitated by first looking up target names in Altham, Godfrey, Mahan, and Rice's (1988) *Index to Personal Names in the National Union Catalog of Manuscript Collections, 1959-1984*. In addition, ask your reference librarian how to gain access to the Research Libraries Information Network (RLIN). RLIN is a useful on-line service that permits users to search for relevant archives by entering target names at a computer terminal.[15]

The result of your search, if you are fortunate, are descriptions of specific, potentially relevant archival collections. The *National Union Catalog of Manuscript Collections* tells you the size of the collection(s)—in linear or cubic feet of material—and the name(s) of the archive(s) where your target's collection(s) is(are) housed. Once a specific collection in a given archive is identified, the next step is to learn more about the archive itself by looking in the *Directory of Archives and Manuscript Repositories in the United States* (National Historical Publications and Records Commission, 1988). Here, you obtain the address and telephone number of the archive as well as other useful information, such as days and hours of operation, special restrictions (if any) on admission, and the titles of published guides to the archive's collections.[16] You can verify the currency of addresses, telephone numbers, and names of archivists in the most recent edition of the *Directory of Special Libraries and Information Centers*.

Ideally, your search nets you a major deposition of papers donated by your target (a primary sedimentation). More likely, however, the *National Union Catalog of Manuscript Collections* directs you via your target's name to papers in someone else's collection (i.e., a secondary sedimentation relative to your target). You might learn, for example, that anthropologist Margaret Mead's papers at the Library of Congress contain several letters to or from your target.

Note carefully, however, that most sizable collections contain letters and documents to, from, or about people, organizations, and topics that are not indexed in RLIN or the *National Union Catalog of Manuscript Collections*. Unless your target was especially famous or well known, RLIN and the *National Union Catalog of Manuscript Collections* may not lead you to useful archival materials via your target's name.[17] If this case fits your situation, your option at this point is to identify archival collections in which there is a high but not certain probability of finding papers to, from, or about your target.

Where might there be papers and materials relevant to your target? Your best guess is the secondary sedimentations of people and organizations associated with your target. To identify these collections, use the names in your master name list to search RLIN or the *National Union Catalog of Manuscript Collections* for large archival deposits of people and organizations associated with your target. You may find several possibilities, and the problem is that you have no way to know if the collections actually contain materials pertaining to your target.

Sad to say, in cases where indexing is superficial or nonexistent, there is no sound alternative but to visit potentially relevant archives and read diligently through likely collections in the hope of finding pertinent documents. Prioritize these collections in terms of potential payoff. Large collections are better bets than smaller collections, all things equal. The collections of large organizations and well-known people are more likely to have detailed finding aids (Chapter 6). People closest to your target and organizations in which your target participated for many years are better gambles than distant relatives or transient associations.

Use common sense when reading descriptions of archival collections. For example, suppose that Professor Alvin Johnson was a close associate of your target from 1914 to 1956, and that your search of the *National Union Catalog of Manuscript Collections* leads you to an archival deposit described as having Johnson's correspondence for 1906-1911. Because the years do not overlap, the Johnson deposit you identified has a low probability of being fruitful for your purposes.

Also consider adding people and organizations to your master name list that have, at this point, logical rather than documented relationships to your target. For example, assume that you know from your master biography file that your target was an early social scientist at the University of Chicago. Your master biography file might not indicate that your target was a close colleague of the first chairperson of the Department of Sociology at the University of Chicago, but it makes logical sense that he or she might have been. Thus, documents concerning your target might reside in the archival papers of that sociology chairperson, Albion Woodbury Small, even if the *National Union Catalog of Manuscript Collections* does not specifically say so.

When searching for secondary archival deposits, be doubly sure to include the names of formal organizations in your systematic probe. Be especially alert for official records of organizations with which the target was closely affiliated. Informative materials may surface in the collections of organization officers, including: membership lists, attendance lists, agendas, official programs, newsletters, committee reports, election files, minutes of executive meetings, award nominations, confidential memos, and other correspondence. A telephone call to the national headquarters of extant associations should quickly reveal the location of an association's archives, if any.

Similarly, the archived records of companies, agencies, schools, and other formal organizations in which the target worked professionally are likely to include evidentiary traces that range from mundane directory information all the way to the target's correspondence and case records, official memos, lecture notes, and promotion file. Presidents' papers at colleges and universities are usually filled with documents relating to faculty members. Many university archives maintain useful biographical files on past professors even if the archives have retained few of their past academics' personal papers per se.

Alternate Search Strategies

For cases in which a target's name is not known, or you are unable to establish the names of people associated with a particular social phenomenon, two alternative research strategies are possible: topical searches and local archive searches. To begin a topical search, you start not with the names of specific individuals but with topical categories, such as: women writers, Russian German immigrants, Army nurses, labor union officials, and so forth. The *Directory of Archives and Manuscript Repositories in the United States* (National Historical Publications and Records Commission, 1988) includes a topic index that identifies archives in terms of topical specializations, but this index should be used with caution. For example, the *Directory* lists literally hundreds of archives that claim archival collections on the general topic of women. Such a list is not sufficiently fine grained to be of much practical help. Simultaneously, the *Directory* lists only two archives claiming collections related to sociology, and thereby seriously underreports the number of deposits relevant to this broad social science topic.

Locating a topical archive appropriate to your interests may require collegial networking. A few telephone calls or letters to scholars who specialize in the history of a given topic area may produce a list of recommended archives.[18] With luck, a topical archive may have caches of letters, diaries, and other documents from which insightful sociobiographical accounts can be constructed that explore a social movement or an institutional sphere of interest to the researcher. But just because you find a relevant topical collection, do not neglect the name-oriented strategy. For example, if you are interested in the playground movement, it behooves you to explore the personal papers of the many people, such as Jane Addams or George Herbert Mead, who were active leaders or social theoreticians in the crusade for more and better playgrounds.

The second alternative, a local search, is simply to make use of materials that are close at hand. The results can be surprising. For example, my research (Hill, 1988a; Hill & Deegan, 1991) on Hattie Plum Williams (the first American woman to chair a coeducational doctoral degree granting program in sociology and political science) began with my reading her files at the local state historical society while looking for data on another topic (see Appendix). Due to the heavy travel costs typically associated with archival research, this strategy makes especially good sense for the novice researcher. Close to home, you can "learn the ropes" of archival procedures at your leisure without draining your savings account.

Students starting their first archival project should seriously consider the local archive strategy. Contact the archivist at your college or university and explain that you would like to undertake a modest archival research project.[19] Ask the archivist or your instructor to suggest a few topics related to the history of your school or your major department. You might, for example, begin by documenting a particular social science professor's activities and accomplishments from 1900 to 1910. Or you might document the social aspects of football during the 1930s. Or you might explore the political positions advocated by social science professors at campus rallies, at faculty meetings, and in campus newspapers during World War I. The possibilities are endless; they depend only on your imagination and your local resources. A crucial point, however, is to keep the project modest in scope so you do not get bogged down in more detail than you can handle.

The geographical arrangement of the *Directory of Archives and Manuscript Repositories in the United States* (National Historical Publications and Records Commission, 1988) lists the names of the major archival repositories in your local area. The pragmatic formula is: Choose a convenient archive and let its holdings dictate your research project. With luck, a nearby archive will have a collection of at least one person's papers that are fully suitable for sociobiographical purposes. Other collections will surely contain materials that can usefully illuminate the institutional fabric and social history of the region in which the researcher lives, works, and writes.

Contacts to Make Before You Visit an Archive

With the possible exception of local archives, it is very important to contact a curator at any archive before you make the actual trip. This precaution pays dividends in averted frustrations and time and money saved. Make a call or write a letter of introduction in which you succinctly outline your project and express your interest in particular collections. Ask the archivist to estimate the number of items in the collection that relate directly to your target or topic, and ask whether the specified collections are open to you. Inquire if copies of relevant finding aids can be obtained for you to study prior to your trip. If you know the tentative dates for your planned visit, ask if your plans are convenient. Inquire whether the curator knows of any related collections that might be useful. If asked, many curators will provide lodging suggestions. The typical response is a brief letter from the archivist stating his or her assessment of the relevance of the collection(s) to your project, together with an invitation to visit.

In deciding whether to spend your money visiting a distant archive, consider obtaining expert advice beyond that provided by archivists per se. If you discovered published works on your target during your literature review, check the footnotes and bibliographies for assessments of potentially relevant archives. It may be useful to contact established scholars and ask their guidance, remembering that they may steer you away from materials they are "saving" for themselves and may, if you give too much away, beat you to the archive and "steal your thunder" when you innocently let a truly super research idea too soon out of the bag. Archivists can usually provide the names of one or two scholars who have already read particular collections, and it may benefit you to confer with the latter. Such scholars may be able to respond to direct questions, such as, "Do you recall any letters to, from, or about Mary Richards in the collection?" Be alert, however, to disciplinary differences and biases when weighing another's overall assessment of a collection.[20]

Pragmatically, let me emphasize that archival research is very often a self-financed labor of love. Principal expenditures are due to the cost of travel and photocopies. There are small grant programs for archival research, but taking the time to complete applications for small grants can be more bother than benefit—and humanities scholars on grant committees are sometimes chary about including social scientists in the distribution of already scarce funds. Self-financing your research avoids placing you in debt to benefactors and lets you set your own research agenda and timetable. Archival research trips can take you to delightful cities, quaint university towns, and foreign countries. With planning, good tax advice, and a briefcase full of receipts, your travel costs may be tax-deductible as professional expenses (a happy result that requires no grant proposals and may be just as remunerative).

NOTES

1. The term *target* is used here to avoid confusion between *subject*, *topic*, and librarians' technical use of the term *subject heading*.

2. For a useful introduction to the formal literature review process in the social sciences, consult Bart and Frankel (1981) or any of the excellent, discipline-specific guides recommended by Sheehy (1986).

3. You can search an updated version of the *National Union Catalog* on-line through OCLC, and *Dissertation Abstracts International* can be searched on-line and on CD-ROM. Check with your local reference librarian for assistance.

4. For a list of discipline-specific abstracts and periodical indexes, consult Sheehy (1986).

5. See Sheehy (1986) for specific suggestions.

6. Sociologists, in particular, should scour the early volumes of the *Papers and Proceedings of the American Sociological Society*. Some articles were reprinted in the *American Journal of Sociology*, but others were not. The *Papers and Proceedings* also include early ASS membership rosters and ASS committee reports.

7. As more than a few early social scientists attracted interest in the humanities, it is sometimes worthwhile to check the *Combined Retrospective Index to Book Reviews in Humanities Journals, 1802-1974*.

8. *BioBase* is available on microfiche in many libraries.

9. A one-volume *Index* to the *National Cyclopædia of American Biography* was published in 1984, which makes it a snap to find biographies in this otherwise overwhelming resource.

10. Greenwood Press of Westport, Connecticut, is currently publishing a large number of biographical dictionaries having considerable relevance to the social sciences.

11. Hint: Annotate each listing with brief identifying comments, such as "second cousin," "paternal uncle," "brother-in-law," "anthropology professor at Harvard, colleague, and co-author," "employer, 1892-1895," and so forth.

12. For example, the Luther L. Bernard Papers at Pennsylvania State University contain many letters and documents that Bernard solicited and collected for use in his writings about the history and development of sociology.

13. For an instructive account of a woman who worked professionally under many different names as a result of marriage and divorce, see Deegan's (1991, pp. 100-109) biography of Mary Elizabeth Burroughs Roberts Smith Coolidge.

14. Do not confuse the *National Union Catalog*, the printed book catalog of the Library of Congress, with the *National Union Catalog of Manuscript Collections*.

15. If your reference librarian is unfamiliar with RLIN, suggest consulting the *Information Industry Directory* (1992), Vol 1, p. 1087.

16. For example, the *Holdings List of the U.S. National Archives and Records Administration* (Davis, 1988) orients you to the myriad collections in the U.S. National Archives in Washington, D.C. Such guides, when available, may tell you about related collections that may be useful to your project.

17. You may come up empty-handed because your target's papers have been donated to an archive but not yet processed. Some archives have huge backlogs. A few archives permit researchers to comb through boxes of unprocessed materials; others do not. If you suspect that your target's papers are in limbo somewhere between donation and formal processing, gamble on writing letters of inquiry to a few likely repositories. Surviving relatives, if you can locate them, may also know where an unprocessed cache of papers is hiding. Searching through unprocessed material can be extremely time-consuming and should be contemplated only if you have extraordinary patience, a well-developed sense of archival intuition, and the luck of the leprechauns.

18. You will have identified the leading scholars in your background literature search. To obtain addresses, check the *National Faculty Directory* or write to the author in care of the applicable publisher. Publishers' addresses are found in the current edition of *Books in Print*.

19. College and university instructors who plan to assign student projects that require archival research should first contact their local archive to discuss the assignment and its potential for overloading the resources of the archive and its archivist. The archivist may want to explain the house rules to all of your students at one time, may want students to consolidate projects to reduce the number of collections involved, may want to limit the number of students who use the archive at any one time, and so on. It is simply prudent, and good manners, to coordinate your teaching plans with local archivists.

20. I once consulted a prominent scholar who assured me that I would find "very little" in a collection that turned out to be a gold mine from a sociologist's point of view. If your work is innovative, archivists and other scholars may tell you your project is unrealistic principally because they lack your perspective.

5. ORIENTATION INTERVIEWS

Upon arrival at an archive, there is an important and usually mandatory interaction ritual (Goffman, 1967): the *orientation interview* (Tissing, 1984). This social interaction, like so many others, typically involves interactants holding differential claims to power, status, and resources (Deegan & Hill, 1987). The archivist occupies an interactional position of considerable power, much of it structural (Chapter 3), which novice investigators do not always appreciate. An orientation interview is a face-to-face encounter with a specific archivist who may literally hold the keys to your research success.

During this crucial interaction ritual, the archivist is introduced to the researcher, and vice versa. If you are a novice, it facilitates matters if you are introduced face-to-face by a researcher already well-known to the archivist. Alternatively, presenting a letter of introduction also helps to establish your legitimacy as a serious scholar. It is especially important to impress upon the archivist your interest in learning and complying with the archive's rules for handling materials in the reading room (Chapter 7). As Philip Brooks (1969) noted, "the more clearly [the patron] understands the responsibilities to care for the materials" (p. 36), the better.

The formality and depth of orientation interviews vary depending on the archive and the archivist: The interview may be casual, folksy, and disarming; friendly and professional; or stiff, pretentious, and needlessly prolonged. Whatever the archivist's presentation of self (Goffman, 1959), researchers should try to establish a cordial yet serious and thoroughly professional persona. It is important to frame these interactions as interviews because archivists base their decisions about access and subsequent services almost wholly on these initial conferences. The old adage about first impressions being important was never more true than here! Whatever the tone, format, or depth, the orientation interview must be successfully negotiated to gain access to archival resources. Brooks (1969) correctly observed, albeit from the perspective of an archivist, that "success in consulting primary sources depends upon the cooperation of the researcher and the archivist" (p. 36). Researchers who botch orientation interviews may seriously disable their research projects.

During the ideal orientation interview, researchers explain their projects, seek the archivist's advice and expertise, request access to presumably relevant materials, and ask for an orientation to reading room procedures, including how to request or page materials and how to order or make photocopies.

It is crucial, when explaining your project, to avoid social science jargon. As Brooks (1969) put it, "the better the prospective user can explain his needs . . . the better the result" (p. 36). Simultaneously, in the ideal interview, the archivist welcomes you, directs you to finding aids, explains local protocols, inquires about your topic and your progress to date, advises you about relevant materials and collections, and, for good measure, recommends a local restaurant or two.

Below the surface of the ideal orientation interview, an unspoken drama of considerable consequence unfolds. The archivist frames the researcher's presentation of self (Goffman, 1959, 1974). Is the researcher legitimate? Is she a potential thief? Will she use the documents carefully? Did she carefully read the archive's "house rules" before she signed the application for admission? Does the researcher "know her business?"[1] Is this an important scholar who should be courted, or a dithering assistant professor who putters unproductively? Should she be helped or allowed to flounder? Is her end product (a proposed book, thesis, or article) worth bothering about? What is the payoff for the archive if the researcher is admitted and staff time diverted from other projects?

Simultaneously, the researcher frames the archivist. Is he helpful, indifferent, or purposefully obstructive? Is he knowledgeable? How fully does he understand the nature and significance of my project? Is he trying to dissuade me from using materials without reasonable justification? Is he sexist, racist, or homophobic? Does he appreciate my time and budget constraints? Researchers must be reflexive, of course, and remember that first appearances can be deceiving.

To the extent that archivists are specialists, they have professional self-images to maintain. Interactionally, researchers should allow for the possibility that the archivist is attempting, during the interview, to present a good face (Goffman, 1967), as when Brooks (1969), himself an archivist, asserts, "a competent archivist is to be looked upon as a scholarly colleague of the researcher, far more than solely a preserver and a caretaker" (p. 36). Although Brooks is obviously correct (a competent archivist is truly a treasure), researchers are advised to recall archivist Maynard Brichford's (1980) sobering observation that "college and university archives embody a variety of intellectual experiences and are affected with a strong taint of amateurism" (p. 453). In short, be mindful of professional posturing that masks something less than archival proficiency.

Although an archive houses an organization's most rare and unique materials, there is no guarantee whatsoever that the archival staff is in fact competent to help you further your project beyond the bureaucratic bare minimum of trying to locate specifically what you ask for. Frank Burke (1981), an archivist, rails against the fragmentary training of many archivists:

> We have the two-week institute; the non-credit traveling workshop; the credit-earning but often discredited 3-credit "archives course" patched into a library curriculum to provide the students with "scope"; the officially sanctioned professional curriculum that concentrates on the practicum as the core of the training, thus assuring the student of "stack rat" status from the beginning; the uncoordinated parade of "instructors" (with no common syllabus, lecture approach, or standards), to which most archival students are subjected in the plethora of jury-rigged institutes. (p. 45)

Judging whether a pleasant, apparently helpful stack rat who has been to a noncredit, 2-week archives institute constitutes, in Brooks's terms, a "competent archivist" who is "to be looked upon as a scholarly colleague" is an interactional framing task of no little import for one's research.

Archivists, like other professionals, vary widely in knowledge and interaction skills. Many archivists have preconceived notions about the social sciences that may confound your best efforts to explain the scope, purpose, and methodological rationale of your proposed study. Persons inquiring about sociology, for example, are sometimes directed immediately to materials on social workers, welfare programs, social security, family counseling, psychology, urban planning, and vice versa. This result is, in some cases, symptomatic of a more general phenomenon. Conway (1986) notes the "continuing reluctance of the archival profession to develop a better understanding of users" (p. 393). Archivists have their own professional culture (Kecskemeti, 1987) and it may work at cross-purposes to your research interests. Materials that an archivist or historian evaluates as useless or uninformative may hold invaluable riches for a social scientist. In any event, be prepared to educate your archivist—patiently, collegially, and without condescension.

The unspoken, mutual framing activity during the initial interview sets the tone and character of subsequent interactions. It determines whether the researcher is given special help by the archivist and staff. If archivists become interested in researchers' projects, they may actively search for data that researchers would not otherwise find or suggest looking at important supplementary materials that researchers might otherwise neglect. If, however, the archivist is disinterested or frames the researcher as an annoyance, important data may remain locked in the vault, never reaching the unwitting researcher.

The archivist's and researcher's initial framings of each other are, of course, vulnerable to reframing (Goffman, 1974). If researchers make only superficial use of numerous and large requests for materials or expand archival searches into areas not stipulated during the initial interview, the archivist may reasonably question "What is going on here?" Conversely, if an archivist entertained initial reservations about a researcher's intentions, these may be dispelled if the investigator exhibits system and purpose when using requested materials, handles the materials carefully, meticulously follows the archive's rules, and asks the archivist astute, informed questions during the course of the archive visit. Simultaneously, researchers' estimates of archivists often change during the course of archive visits, sometimes discounting an archivist's initial counsel, sometimes concluding that an apparent bumbler has a mind like the proverbial steel trap.

An archivist's professional and organizational interest lies in promoting the use of archived materials by legitimate researchers. Brichford (1980) observes, "archives—repositories and documents—and the archivists who are responsible for them draw their identity from the institutions they serve" (p. 449). Curators are usually delighted if materials in their archives will help advance your scholarly agenda. As a courtesy, make it a point to record the full names and official titles of the curators and full-time staff who assist or advise you in archives for later acknowledgment in your publications. In addition, your future correspondence with the archive following your visit is facilitated if you keep a list of names, addresses, and telephone numbers.

NOTES

1. When an archivist asks, "Where else have you looked?" you are being asked to display your preparation for your visit in terms of (a) searching for and reading relevant published works and (b) your familiarity with and experiences in other archives.

6. CONFRONTING THE "BLACK BOX" PROBLEM

Archives are essentially large "black boxes" from which you must extract useful data without being able to look directly inside. Having identified and arrived at an archive, your first tasks are: (a) to locate and request specific items and/or boxes of materials in promising collections, and (b) to identify additional collections in the archive that may prove useful. There are three ways to locate materials in most archives: peruse the archive's general catalog, consult finding aids for specific collections, and request the archivist's informed suggestions. These options prove straightforward in some cases, but in others the black box situation is close to intractable.

The General Catalog

The general catalog is the principal key to the overall contents of an archive. Indeed, the archivist typically consults the general catalog (usually located in the reading room) on your behalf during the orientation interview. The catalog looks physically in appearance much like the now old-fashioned card catalogs in most libraries,[1] but there the similarity ends. Archives are not arranged on standardized schemes (such as the Dewey decimal system or the Library of Congress classification) commonly used to uniquely categorize books and organize libraries. An intriguing and sometimes frustrating aspect of using an archive is its distinctive and idiosyncratic character, and the general catalog reflects these idiosyncrasies. What gets entered in the general catalog—and what does not—depends on the interests, mandates, and resources of past and present curators.

The organization of libraries is based on cataloging discrete, easily identifiable objects (i.e., books), whereas archives are arranged in terms of collections, each of which may hold hundreds of thousands (and sometimes millions) of separate items such as letters and other documents. While books in libraries are typically identified by at least three entries (i.e., author, title, subject) in library catalogs, it is usually impracticable to separately catalog each item in archival collections. This fact makes the task of requesting archival materials much more problematic than looking up a book in your local library.

At a minimum, the general catalog is an alphabetical index to the names of the persons and organizations whose papers or collections reside in the archive. A collection is typically a set of more or less heterogeneous materials associated with a person or organization, after whom the collection is usually named.[2] Government and some university archives are wholly or partially organized along bureaucratic lines, that is, by names of departments, commissions, agencies, and so forth. The extent to which materials in each collection are subclassified, individually cataloged, and cross-referenced in the general catalog is peculiar to each archive.

Comprehensive inventory and cataloging are expensive, time-consuming, and well beyond the resources of many archives. The general catalog might itemize the names of all correspondents in a highly prized collection on which a curator has lavished a great deal of time. For other collections, however, the general catalog includes only the names of "major" correspondents. For still other collections, no correspondents are listed by name in the general catalog. Note that very few collections are likely to be cataloged by topic, even in rudimentary fashion. At best, the general catalog is a rough, uneven guide to an archive's contents— but it should never be ignored.

Finding Aids

A finding aid provides a brief one- or two-page scope statement (or description) of an archival collection, accompanied by an outline of the structural organization of the collection and a more or less detailed inventory of the items in the collection. Some archives publish elaborate finding aids for especially treasured collections, but, more often, finding aids are typewritten and placed in notebook binders. The finding aids are usually housed together in the archive's reading room in file cabinets or open shelves where you can consult them freely. When a particularly massive collection is inventoried item by item, the results are sometimes kept in separate card files similar to the archive's general catalog.

The most common finding aid is a simple box list, that is, a summary inventory of the contents of each storage box in which the materials of a collection are physically placed. The information in typical box list entries is similar to these examples: "Box 5, Incoming correspondence, A-H, 1921-1922"; "Box 22, Unpublished manuscripts"; "Boxes 40-44, Student papers"; "Boxes 60-87, Pamphlet collection on social reform"; "Box 100, Diaries, 1905-1907, 1934-1946"; and so on. Relatively more comprehensive finding aids, on the other hand, feature item-by-item inventories of virtually every document in a collection. The inventory may be chronologically arranged but is often alphabetically ordered by names of correspondents. If you are fortunate, the finding aids for the collections you need to use will feature alphabetical lists of all documents and correspondents together with the date and file location of each document.

Comprehensive aids typically list items by who wrote or received a document rather than by the people or topics discussed in a document. For example, if Professor George Herbert Mead wrote a letter of reference on behalf of his student Jessie Taft, Taft's name would probably not appear in the finding aid or collection description. If you want to gamble that Mead wrote such a letter, and kept a file copy, then to find it you would need to skim through all of Mead's correspondence for the pertinent years. Likewise, if you want to locate every letter in the Mead Papers in which Professor Mead discussed political economy, women's rights, or the rationale for establishing schools of philanthropy, then you will probably have to read all of Mead's correspondence.

Try to obtain copies of any published finding aids for the major collections that you anticipate using during a forthcoming archival trip. Archives often distribute their published finding aids, usually for a fee. Copies may even be available in local libraries. If you offer to pay, archivists will usually make photocopies of typewritten finding aids and mail them to you. The expense may seem high, but compared to the cost of an archival trip per se, the cost is usually negligible. Studying a finding aid helps you decide whether a planned archiving trip is worth it or not.

It takes time to carefully examine a lengthy finding aid and decide what materials to request in what sequence. It is better to do this work at home rather than at an out-of-town archive where living expenses are higher and time is literally money. When you travel to a distant archive, pack your copies of relevant finding aids. You can pore over them each night in your hotel room and map out your box requests for the next day.

Seeking the Archivist's Advice

If you did your homework (Chapter 4), you will arrive at an archive with a specific collection in mind. But an archive that has useful materials in one collection frequently contains additional items of interest in other collections, collections that you will want to identify during your visit. For example, if your target was a university faculty member, items of interest may reside in a large number of collections within the university's archives, such as the collections of colleagues, administrators, academic departments, scientific clubs, faculty senates, boards of regents or governors, and so on. But you have to discover these collections before you can use them. You might discover relevant additional collections by systematically looking up names from your master name list in the archive's general catalog, or by canvassing the available finding aids. More often than not, however, you will learn about related collections by asking the resident archivist for guidance.

The archivist's knowledge of the collections is especially crucial when the general catalog and finding aids provide little information about the specific contents of a collection or when your interest is primarily topical. The archivist may be able to shorten the search process and lead you directly to useful materials.

Confronting and Minimizing Archival Errors:
Type II and Type I

Archivists sometimes present themselves as thoroughly knowledgeable about the contents and significance of certain collections.[3] In such instances, the archivist may lead researchers immediately to useful materials, or counsel that the collection has little to offer. Both responses may be accurate. On the other hand, there may be much more in a given collection that is actually useful to your research than the archivist perceives. Conversely, the archivist may assert that "there is much that should be of interest" in a given collection when the opposite is the case. Do the archivists know whereof they speak? If they do, researchers are saved hours of fruitless searching. If they do not, researchers can be inadvertently misled.

It is not far wrong to conceptualize each archive as a warehouse of unknowable size stocked with innumerable boxes, each filled with a large array of individual items which may or may not be adequately inventoried and cataloged. In an ideal world, researchers simply bulldoze the dilemma of choosing items to examine by systematically consulting every potentially useful file, letter, or document. In using the Archives of the History of American Psychology, for example, Popplestone (1975) advised: "The ability of the archival staff to serve the historian is directly correlated with both the specificity and breadth of requests. For maximum yield the student should enumerate all individuals whose papers might have relevant data. The key words in this guideline are *individual* and *all*" (p. 22). Good advice, but if time is limited, as it almost always is, researchers are increasingly dependent on the archivist's professed expertise and knowledge. Since you cannot read everything, you must make choices, and in so doing you run a considerable risk of making an error.

As researchers' resources become constrained through lack of time and/or money, the problem facing researchers increasingly obtains the characteristics of a socially mediated "game" (Leinfellner, 1976) in which researchers try to maximize archival payoff while limiting losses of time and energy. This situation is conceptually similar to the problem of estimating the risk of making an error in statistical inference.

To statisticians, *"the error of failing to reject an hypothesis when it is actually false,* is referred to as a *type II or Beta error"* (Blalock, 1972, p. 113). Accepting an archivist's judgment that a given collection has no relevant material, when in fact it does, is the logical equivalent of a type II error. Conversely, electing to read dutifully through a collection that an archivist assures the researcher will be helpful, but is not, is also an error of this type.

At the same time, "we also run the risk of making another kind of error, that of *rejecting a true hypothesis.* We refer to this kind of error as a *type I or alpha error"* (Blalock, 1972, p. 114). Stubbornly searching a collection that the archivist has correctly advised will be of little use is the logical equivalent of a type I error. Conversely, skeptically disregarding an archivist's correct advice to read a collection that would in fact be very helpful is also an error of the same type.

There is, unfortunately, no way to avoid these potential errors in the real world of limited budgets and bureaucratic schedules, but seasoned researchers try to maximize archival payoffs while minimizing unproductive wild goose chases. When time is limited, experienced researchers concentrate their efforts on: (a) large collections of known or highly probable relevance to the research project, and (b) collections in well-staffed, professionally run archives with sophisticated archivists and detailed finding aids that help to quickly limit searches to materials of high potential utility to the project at hand.

As time and resources permit, however, practiced researchers expand their searches to additional archives and more marginal collections. A single archive is rarely adequate to the iterative, hermeneutic requirements of solid archival investigation. Brooks (1969) observed, "There are practically no topics of major research (that is, say, of the scope of a doctoral dissertation) that can be studied adequately in one repository of papers" (p. 45). An archival study based on materials from a single repository runs an especially high risk of factual inadequacy and intellectual distortion.

Summary

Three methods for accessing archival materials are discussed above: checking names in general catalogs, consulting finding aids, and asking archivists for suggestions. With practice, you will no doubt become an astute researcher who uses all three methods effectively, but you can never avoid the practical possibility of making errors. For example, the name entry "Pound, Roscoe" in the general catalog of one archive cross-referred this researcher to a collection containing several Pound letters, but the same archive also housed another collection holding an equally significant number of Pound letters that were not cross-referenced in the catalog under Pound's name. The existence of the letters in the second collection was discovered only through studying the finding aids of collections that I thought might be useful. In another archive, I was eventually brought a stack of boxes brimming with materials belonging to a nationally prominent scholar. The materials had not been inventoried and there was no entry for the materials in the general catalog. There was no finding aid. I was led to these materials only after seeking the archivist's informed suggestions. In both cases, I discovered materials that documented previously unknown facts about Roscoe Pound and sociological jurisprudence. It is impossible, of course, to estimate how many other deposits of Pound materials I narrowly missed even though I consulted general catalogs, studied the appropriate finding aids, and asked archivists for their suggestions.

NOTES

1. Card catalogs are disappearing as libraries shift to computerized systems. In future, expect the eventual transfer of archival catalogs to machine readable formats that can be consulted on-line in the archive or from across the country. The Special Collections Department at Stanford University, for example, has already taken significant steps in this direction.

2. In rare instances, collections are composed of materials specially assembled under a topical subject heading of interest to an archivist. For an interesting example of a topical collection, see the "Ross Controversy Papers" at Stanford University. This collection pulls together a series of documents related to the controversial dismissal of economist and sociologist Edward A. Ross from Stanford in 1900.

3. For that matter, so do many researchers who claim to have "read" particular collections.

7. LIFE IN THE READING ROOM

Archival materials are consulted by researchers in a designated reading room, often at an assigned table space reserved specially for this use. Here, you fill out request slips to have specific boxes retrieved and brought to you for your examination. This chapter outlines the main features of research in an archival reading room, including interactional ambiguity, reading room protocols, and the importance of requesting and/or making photocopies. The discussion concludes with observations on using microfilms and hiring surrogate investigators.

The reading room is often occupied by other researchers engrossed in their separate projects. Some reading rooms are Spartan, others are richly appointed with leather-covered chairs, Persian carpets, walnut paneling, and stained glass windows. Whatever the physical appearance, however, the reading room is a place for absolute quiet and studious concentration. The archive reading room is virtually a "sacred space" for many scholars (Goffman, 1967).

Social interactions in the reading room are sometimes frustrating and ambiguous, and complicated by the bureaucratic organization of archives. You must learn to work with the feeling that someone is always watching you—because someone almost always is. You will typically be kept under constant surveillance in a modern "panopticon" (Foucault, 1979, pp. 195-228) by the archivist or the archivist's staff assistants (and, in some instances, by uniformed, armed guards). It is important to pay attention to your feelings in the research setting and to reflexively consider how they may affect your work (Reinharz, 1984).

Infighting between the archivist and the staff can catch researchers in the cross fire. It is the reading room assistants who usually retrieve materials for you from the stacks, and they can purposefully blockade your work or go "all out" to help. Requests for materials from the vault can be filled quickly in minutes, or take several long hours. If your time is severely limited, unexplained delays in receiving requested materials are particularly frustrating. But you must learn to "keep your cool" if you want the continued help of the archivist and the staff, however incompetent and slow that help might be.

Experientially, researchers can be immobilized by interactional ambiguity during the course of an archival visit. For example, staff assistants may seem to studiously ignore you, or respond with pained expressions when you request materials and submit photocopy applications. The archivist, for no apparent reason, may ask if your research is "just about done" when you have only scratched the surface of the available materials. You may question whether you continue to be welcomed, or if you presented yourself appropriately during the orientation interview. Such ongoing interactional ambiguities can prompt researchers to ask themselves,

"What is going on here?" and, if asked too frequently, generate "negative experience" (Goffman, 1974). You must be careful not to let these questions become so intrusive that your work is disrupted.

Productive examination and analysis of archival documents is an acquired skill. Novices frequently delve through a box of documents only to conclude, "There is nothing here." The old hand, given the same material, gasps, "Oh my, do you know what this means!" Discerning sociohistorical significance or patterns in, for example, old letters, tattered receipts, yellowed lecture notes, cryptic diary entries, or files of canceled checks requires iterative contemplation of the archival record as a whole. The value of particular bits of data or evidence ebbs and flows as your understanding of a target's life story grows in complexity and insight. Meaning emerges from reading the contents of an archival file not once, but several times during the course of a project (Chapter 9).

Reading Room Protocols

Each archive reading room is a singular place with special rules. In reading rooms across the country, irreplaceable empirical traces of the past will be temporarily placed in your custody for you to study. Whatever else can be said about using archives, nothing is more important than emphasizing your responsibility to handle these materials with the utmost care and respect. Most archives have developed specific house rules or protocols that describe precisely what you may and may not do in the reading room. These rules might sometimes seem arcane, but they are designed to address one paramount concern—the protection and preservation of archival documents. You have no business in an archive if you cannot commit yourself absolutely to this concern both in spirit and in your actions.

Be alert to the fact that reading room protocols vary in detail from archive to archive. For a variety of reasons, permissible behavior in one archive may be verboten in another. Ignoring these differences will certainly bring stern reprimands, and possibly your immediate expulsion from an archive. Not all archives advise every patron about expected behaviors. This does not excuse you from using common sense, however. If you are not given an orientation about local rules, then ask the archivist if there are any special reading room procedures. If you do not understand the rules or procedures, ask to have rules repeated and procedures demonstrated.

If at any time during your visit you wonder if a particular action is permissible, ask before you do it.

Some reading room rules are universal, or nearly so. Writing or making marks or erasures of any kind on archival documents is strictly prohibited in all archives. Willful acts of theft and vandalism are everywhere intolerable and illegal. Ink pens and ballpoint pens are banned in most archives, so be sure to bring your own pencils. Keep your hands clean, as dirty fingerprints hasten the disintegration of paper documents. If you have the sneezes, take effective medication, or else stay away from the archives. Do not touch your face or hair and then touch a document. Never bring food, snacks, beverages, chewing gum, or candies into a reading room. Most archives provide lockers and request that you store your personal belongings therein. Many archives allow you to bring your own note cards into the reading room, but a few even provide the paper on which you can take notes. Some archives allow the use of portable computers; others do not.

All archives require that you return materials in exactly the same order that you received them. Be very careful never to overturn a storage box or spill the contents of a file folder. If you do have an accident, consult the archivist about how to put the documents back in their original order; do not try to guess what that order might be. If you inadvertently put a document in the wrong box or file folder, it may be effectively lost for decades, or possibly forever. Never open more than one storage box at a time, and never remove more than one file folder at a time from a storage box. Observe local protocols to properly guard materials during your absence if you leave the reading room for any reason, and never leave materials unattended lying open exposed to light. As you read through the materials in a file folder, lay the folder flat on the table in front of you, carefully turning over one sheet at a time. Do not rest your arms or elbows on the documents. Never disturb the sequence of the materials in a file folder. If you see an item that you think is misfiled (that is, not in what seems to be the apparent chronological or alphabetical sequence), call the situation to the archivist's attention. Under no circumstances should you take it upon yourself to correct what appears to you to be an error.

Fragile materials can literally fall apart in your hands if you are not very, very careful. If you suspect that an item is too fragile to handle, ask the archivist for help. If you encounter a document that is stapled or pinned together, do not bend, fold, or tear the document. Conversely, do not try to "iron out" or flatten deeply creased documents. Do not remove staples or straight pins, or open sealed envelopes, without the permission of the archivist. In short, treat every document with respect.

Making and Reading Photocopies

It is a bit misleading today to refer to "reading" a collection when investigators visit an archive. Seasoned researchers rarely pore over each letter or take detailed notes on what they read while they are at an archive per se. Rather, they learn to skim collections for relevant or useful documents and then have them photocopied. You may eventually invest several hundreds of dollars in photocopies, but these are usually a bargain compared to the expense required for extended or repeated archival visits.

There are many advantages to using photocopies. Photocopies can be physically reorganized and sorted into topical categories at a researcher's whim. Letters from different correspondents and archives can be combined and read side by side. You can study relaxed, with a cup of coffee in one hand and a sandwich in the other. Your personal files of photocopies are, in fact, a small private archive to which you can return at will, and continually expand through further research.[1] Researchers sometimes share photocopies, although this is discouraged by most archives.[2] The considered, iterative sifting of materials takes place at your home office where photocopies of documents from a variety of archives can be consulted together.

Whatever you read or photocopy, be absolutely certain to systematically note the name of the collection, the box number, and the file folder in which the original document is located. You will need this information to properly document your sources when you prepare your study for publication or your thesis committee. If you do not correctly identify a document, you may never be able to relocate it without redoing all your archival work and you may never be able to cite this information (Chapter 10).

The greatest variation in reading room protocols is in policies and methods for requesting and making photocopies of archival documents. No two archives employ precisely identical procedures. Typically, however, there is (a) a request form on which you must fully describe the items to be copied, and (b) a system for identifying or flagging the documents to be copied. In most repositories, the archivist must approve your request. Advance payment is often required, sometimes not.[3] Photocopies are made by the archive staff and then mailed to you. Occasionally, however, photocopy requests are filled and delivered prior to the conclusion of your archival stay. Whenever you receive your copies, annotate each sheet with the archive's name, the collection's name, and the correct box and folder number.

A few archives not only permit but encourage self-service photocopying.[4] This approach reduces demands on staff time, provides you with virtually instant photocopies of documents, and is usually less costly on a per copy basis. You may need to obtain permission before making each photocopy, however. Furthermore, you will probably be competing with other researchers to use the available photocopy machines. In general, the demand for self-service copiers is lowest early in the day, but as closing time approaches the pressure on the machines can become severe, and you may be unable to copy documents that are central to your study. Some archives allow you to reserve blocks of time at photocopy machines; others have no formal limit on how long a patron can "hog" a copier. Most archives that permit self-service copying will also copy documents for you on request, but at a considerably higher cost per copy. But that cost may be the more economical in the long run if it frees up precious archival research time from the mechanical but time-consuming routine of photocopying. If there is no option but to make your own copies, organize your work and allocate your time carefully.

The greatest number of reading room protocol violations probably occurs in connection with photocopying, especially where self-service copying is permitted. Thus, be especially careful when handling materials to make copies. Pace your work and do not try to do more than you can do carefully. It can be a disaster if you get in a hurry and become careless, irritable, or flustered.

Reading Microfilms

Microfilms of several major archival collections are now available, and new collections are added yearly. Before you go to the expense of travel to an archive, always inquire if the materials you want to use are available on microfilm. Conversely, if you prefer to make a trip to use the original documents rather than a microfilm, call first. Some archives do not permit originals to be consulted once a collection has been filmed. Visiting the archive in such cases may get you little more than you could obtain through interlibrary loan. Some archives will, for a charge, make microfilms on request. The expense is usually high, so be sure you check on the cost before you obligate yourself.

Reading a microfilm has a few disadvantages compared to studying the originals and making photocopies, but the disadvantages are not always significant. Film copies are often less desirable to use for many reasons. Generally, the image of any given document is often less than optimal. As microfilm is literally a strip, you lose the ability to "leaf through" a file, skipping efficiently ahead as is sometimes possible when using the original documents. Omissions are not always annotated. The ability to distinguish the quality of paper on which the original document was written is lost and the ability to distinguish between originals and carbon copies is reduced. Color is lost when filmed in black and white (as is presently typical). Creases or folds in paper sometimes disappear on film copies (making it less obvious that a document may have been an enclosure folded up within another document). Pagination sequences on "folded note" stationery (unless carefully numbered) are more difficult to decipher. Some researchers report eye strain when reading microfilms. You need access to a good microfilm reader (you can find the machines in most libraries, but they are often in poor repair), and if you want paper copies to sort and shift around, you will need access to a microfilm reader-printer.[5] All in all, it is a good deal less fun to read a microfilm than to see and read the original documents firsthand.

Archiving at a Distance

Although it is usually desirable and necessary to visit an archive to do archival research, there are some exceptions. Obviously, you can lessen your travels if microfilm copies of major collections relevant to your project are available locally or through interlibrary loans. Other possibilities include appealing to the archivist for help and hiring a surrogate researcher.

You can always appeal directly to a distant archive and request assistance in obtaining materials. Small and carefully circumscribed requests stand the best chance of success. For example, you may find a footnote in a published study that references a particular letter in a specific archive. If you believe this letter would be especially important to your work, try writing to the appropriate archivist. Briefly explain the potential significance of the letter and carefully identify the document as fully as possible (including date of the letter, who wrote to whom, collection name, and box number and folder designation, if known). It may help to include a photocopy of the source footnote (thus, if the author made an error describing the letter or its archival location, you won't get the blame for sending the archivist on a wild goose chase). Ask if you can obtain a photocopy of the letter, and be sure to state your willingness to pay any associated costs. If the archivist has the time and inclination, you may receive a copy of the letter by return mail without the expense of an archival trip. Because of the many demands on their time, however, you may not receive an answer for several months.

If you need a larger number of documents, your chances of persuading an archivist to make copies for you rapidly diminish. Even so, some archivists are very cooperative if they believe you are serious about your work. It never hurts to ask for help if you do so politely and do not presume to take the archivist's time and service for granted. At the least, most archivists will respond by letter outlining the enormity of the task you propose, together with an invitation to come look for yourself. If you don't get a response, however, follow up with a polite reminder in a note or by telephone.

Archives often operate on shoestring budgets, so that just answering your inquiry is a big task. You should not expect long distance help via the mail when funds and archival personnel are already stretched to the limit. The solution, however, may be to hire a surrogate researcher who will visit a repository on your behalf. Indeed, archivists sometimes suggest this possibility and a few curators are prepared to recommend "approved" researchers for your consideration if you ask.

Surrogate arrangements work best when you have access to a detailed finding aid that inventories the collection document by document. Thus, you can specifically identify each document you want copied. Your surrogate's task is the primarily clerical job of requesting the correct boxes, finding and flagging the items you want copied, completing the photocopy requests, and—in self-service situations—making the copies. This is a gamble to the extent that you will have little if any idea about what is actually in the documents until your photocopies arrive. The whole expense of making telephone calls to interview and hire a surrogate, paying the surrogate (usually by the hour), and reimbursing the archive or the surrogate for the copies made on your behalf may all be for naught, although you have saved the cost of an archiving trip. At the same time, the proposition is risky and you deprive yourself of the firsthand opportunity to examine materials. You might easily pay hundreds of dollars for surrogate research assistance and receive little of any utility to your project. It is best if you examine the contents of archival collections for yourself.

58

NOTES

1. As a last grasp at control, a few archives require patrons to sign agreements promising to return all photocopies once a project is completed. In practice, most sociohistorical projects are cumulative over the lifetime of a scholar's career and never technically reach "completion." Thus, photocopies are rarely returned.

2. Several archives now stamp photocopies with restrictive messages such as "FURTHER REPRODUCTION PROHIBITED WITHOUT WRITTEN PERMISSION." In some cases, however, such material is clearly in the public domain (a clipping of a book review from a 1901 newspaper is a good example), and in other cases archives' proprietary claims are at least arguable. In any event, some photocopy shops timidly balk at recopying any archival photocopy that is emblazoned with a restrictive message.

3. Hint: Personal checks are usually acceptable, but not always. You may need cash, especially at government-run archives or if you are visiting from out of state. One archive required my bank credit card number on the photocopy request form. The copies were subsequently approved, made, and mailed to me—and the fee charged directly to my bank card account.

4. Hint: Obtaining change for photocopy machines is often a headache. Although some archives have automated change machines, most archives do not make change. Call ahead to learn if you will need rolls of coins or small bills. In some repositories, you must buy a machine-readable copycard to insert into the copier—but sometimes you must make this purchase at an inconveniently located business office.

5. The copies produced by older reader-printers are sometimes awful. Newer, plain paper machines are much better—and are usually more expensive. When making copies from microfilms, be sure to identify each copy with the collection name, reel number, and frame number.

8. STRATEGIES FOR ORGANIZING ARCHIVAL DATA

The skill of making sociohistorical sense out of the documents you discover in an archive is fundamentally a process of learning by doing. There are, nonetheless, systematic perspectives to organize your materials and structure your research. These techniques will not mechanically produce flashes of historical insight or intellectual revelation, but they make it easier to see patterns and relationships in the archival record.

What are the techniques for making sense out of archival materials? In practice, the answers are contingent on the nature and content of the archival deposits you discover. Archival analysis is not rigidly fixed, and you learn to extract what you can find. There is enormous room for analytical initiative and innovation in virtually every archival investigation. A few uses of archival data, however, are elemental. Three pragmatic possibilities are discussed in this chapter: (a) spatiotemporal chronologies, (b) networks and cohorts, and (c) backstage perspectives and processes.

Spatiotemporal Chronologies

Every social phenomenon, organization, or movement unfolds over time and space, and you can comb archival deposits to document and reconstruct the spatiotemporal chronology or matrix of sociohistorical events. A preliminary chronology is constructed using dates and places mentioned in published sources, biographical dictionaries, encyclopedias, and the like. Your time-line can never be totally complete, however. Chronologies reflect the necessarily partial data from which each working chronology is constructed. Pragmatically, no chronology can realistically include every small spatiotemporal detail of a subject's life.

Importantly, each chronology reflects the compiler's research experiences, assumptions, convictions, and subsequent decisions about what events to include and what to exclude. Margaret Stieg (1988) astutely notes:

> Good historical research requires a sense of conviction and a point of view. Interpretation and selection go hand in hand; one is the result of the other. The writer must establish a personal relationship with the events being recounted. Where involvement is lacking, the result is not only dull, but it is likely to lack structure, conviction, and proportion; what is important will not be distinguished from what is unimportant. (p. 17)

Researchers systematically and sometimes dramatically vary in what kinds of events they consider to be theoretically and empirically important.

The social sciences pay close attention to the institutional aspects of chronological data, and draw attention to the activities of social groups. We are greatly informed by learning what happens to people in similar circumstances. Sociohistorical research permits institutional forces and group processes to be seen more clearly through their articulation in the lives of individuals in social situations and networks. Sociological interpretation of chronologies is facilitated if researchers take special care to search the archival record for dates of events that document: (a) the target's entry into new roles and institutional arenas, (b) changes in the target's status and/or role(s) within a particular social institution or setting, and (c) the target's involvement in any roles that promote cooperation or conflict within or between distinct institutional spheres.

Archival materials that tell you dates and places are extremely varied. For example: diaries, scrapbooks, clipping service files, birth certificates, baptismal records, licenses, passports, membership cards, school transcripts, bank records, bills, tax returns, court documents, wills, deeds, and mortgage papers are sources of dates (as well as other information). Memorabilia may include invitations, theater programs, or ticket stubs that place people in specific cities on given dates. Packets of "get well" cards may identify the dates of an illness or injury. When reviewing each archival document, ask yourself what it adds factually to your chronological data file.

Letters may reveal when major life decisions about schooling, interpersonal commitments, or lifework were first contemplated, resolved, or later revised. One may learn from a series of letters, for example, that an important book published and ostensibly written by your target in 1926 was, in fact, conceived in 1905, outlined in 1906, and drafted in all its essentials in 1910. Letters may recount when and where enormous efforts were spent on projects that never garnered public notice. It may be possible to date the onset and resolution of personal trials such as mental depression or the tragic loss of significant others. Clues to the temporal rhythm of an individual's domestic work and professional chores may be uncovered in letters written to friends, colleagues, and relatives.

Chronologies can be compiled for organizations as well as for individuals. For example, characteristic aspects of academic departments can be charted temporally, including: enrollments, budget fluctuations, courses taught, arrivals and departures of faculty members, departmental reorganizations, and so forth. Multiple chronologies for similar departments at several colleges and universities can be compiled and compared.[1] Events in professional associations, such as the American Sociological Society/Association (Rhoades, 1981), are also amenable to chronological exposition.

Separate, detailed chronologies of documented events for individuals and organizations can be constructed using temporally arranged 3x5 cards (with no more than one event per card) or entered by date in computer files and updated as new information is acquired. Given sufficiently fine-grained data, entries can also be rearranged to reconstruct annual cycles of significant events. Temporal chronologies can also be keyed to geographical locations and used to construct time-space diagrams. Each chronology is an open-ended research vehicle that you can repeatedly update to articulate the spatiotemporal dimensions of a target's journey through time and space.

Parallel comparisons between the chronologies of several organizations or cohorts of individuals may reveal previously unrecognized spatiotemporal patterns.[2] You might see, for example, that several individuals all made similar personal or career choices at about the same historical moment, or that one person made very different decisions compared to others in his or her professional cohort. For example, which individuals attended the Columbian World's Exposition in Chicago, and which did not? Who went to midwestern public schools, and who to eastern private academies? When and where did each person first present a paper at a professional meeting? Making such comparisons, suggested by events in one or more chronologies, helps identify anomalies and informational gaps in the chronologies of other cohort members. An unexplained temporal gap appearing across all the chronologies of a cohort may point to a basic information deficiency in your initial literature review that you need to repair. Given more complete chronologies, the sophistication of the questions you think to pose and answer is markedly improved.

Networks and Cohorts

Many of the documents that help researchers build chronologies also permit the reconstruction of social and collegial networks. Most sociobiographical targets operated at one time or another in communities, work groups, and/or networks of relatives and professional colleagues, friends and enemies, and formal and informal organizations. Archival data typically help document the nature and extent of complex networks of interpersonal contact, intellectual influence, financial support, political action, organizational affiliations, and so on.

The published proceedings of a professional meeting may tell you who was officially on the program, but letters or other archival documents may tell who was in the audience, or who caucused unofficially with whom. Organizational letterheads are valuable sources of data on officers, committee structures, and terms of office. The minutes, programs, mimeographed handouts, and business meeting agendas of many organizations survive only in archival collections.

Letters exchanged between cohort members typically provide evidence of interpersonal contact. Note, however, that documenting both sides of exchanges of personal and professional letters—even within a small set of correspondents—often requires perseverance and travel to several archival repositories. Thus, be alert to individuals who saved carbon copies of all outgoing correspondence as well as incoming letters. Invitations, calling cards, guest lists, autograph books, and guest books are additional sources that further demonstrate the active workings of social networks. By using the logic of graph theory and network analysis, you may, for example, demonstrate the relative isolation of certain types of professional networks, show previously unrecognized interpersonal links between members of supposedly distinct theory groups, hypothesize and explore the possibility of influential relationships between particular academic departments, or show how specific individuals exemplified various patterns of organizational participation or membership. With sufficient data, the durability of networks over time, as well as changes in shape, composition, and density, may be studied.

Tables or diagrams of interpersonal networks and organizational linkages are major working tools in sociohistorical research. When reading documents in archival collections, keep alert for new linkages and interpersonal contacts, and for data that confirm or reinforce links previously documented. When you discover a new name, always ask, who was that person? What did he or she do? What was the frequency and nature of the connection to my target? Is the person linked in specific ways to other people in my target's interpersonal network? By asking network questions systematically, your records will exhibit increasing complexity, density, and clarity. Your appreciation of previously unrecognized networks can be dramatic. As various networks take shape, they lead researchers back to published sources (such as biographical dictionaries) to read about the projects or study the works published by network members (and to the footnotes and references cited in those works). The relationship between published sources and archival data becomes reciprocal in the best sense.

Backstage Perspectives and Processes

Initial network studies document the existence of organizational and interpersonal ties, but further study of manuscript collections is required to gain insights to the emotional importance and practical meaning of particular network linkages. Intellectual, financial, and moral debts may be acknowledged more fully in private letters than in published prefaces and footnotes. One might learn from a letter, for example, that your target reported being turned more forcefully toward a new intellectual direction by having attended a single public lecture given by a union organizer than by all the scholarly authorities cited by the target in subsequent monographs or public speeches.

But what is the truth status of a writer's assertion in a letter to a friend? Sociologists understand that backstage performances are neither more "real" nor inherently more true than front stage presentations (Goffman,

1959). Researchers must confront questions of motive and validity in both cases, and these are not always easily resolved. The point is that both perspectives are required if a sociohistorical account is to be drawn adequately rather than superficially.

Manuscript collections typically include backstage reflections or remarks that differ markedly in tone, detail, and apparent candor from those intended for publication. Correspondence with friends, family members, and trusted colleagues often reveal specific personal preferences and professional judgments. Memoranda, diaries, marginal notes in books, and observational journals, for example, may reveal the pattern of a scholar's research habits. Careful perusal of letters of reference, grade books, comments on student papers, or confidential prepublication reviews of other scholars' manuscripts allows you to outline the biases and evaluative standards employed by your target in everyday life. Firsthand accounts and opinions not only help establish the work patterns and axiological dimensions (Hill, 1984) of an individual's career, they also bring vitality and animation when quoted in sociohistorical writing.

Front stage images presented in publications and official press releases are the visible points of complex backstage processes that can be documented and analyzed using archival data. Patterns of editorial process come alive in letters between authors and publishers, and in files of rejected manuscripts. A thoughtful review of unfunded grant applications may tell more about a federal agency or philanthropic foundation than does an inventory of the projects they approved. Transcripts of "closed door" meetings may demonstrate whether a professional organization is run democratically or by a clique. Letters of reference and organizational files on candidates for jobs, tenure, and promotion reveal backstage processes that culminate in advancement for a few and in rejection for many more. Court testimony, depositions given to investigators, and confidential reports on organizational disputes provide backstage access to conflicts and power struggles that surface in public with very different faces. Significantly, archival research on backstage processes can enlighten politically disenfranchised minorities and unmask the mystery that covers discriminatory practices.

NOTES

1. See, for example, the appendices in Harvey (1987, pp. 222-293), but note Deegan's (1990) critical appraisal of Harvey's compilations.

2. See, for example, the illuminating charts in Deegan (1988a, pp. 16, 76, 131, 133-134, 135, 162, 164, 216-217, 287, 321, 324).

9. METHODOLOGICAL COMPLEXITIES

Making sense of archival data is an iterative process in which researchers organize and impute meaning to the archival strip through repeated reconsideration of older data combined with the constant infusion of new data. The intellectual and historical significance of archival materials shifts continually during the process of investigation. Through iterative framing, researchers move beyond recognizing a particular letter as interesting in itself to frame it as part of an evolving sociohistorical picture. This process is the culminating phase of archival research.

When you open a box of archival documents, you confront a "raw batch of occurrences," to borrow Erving Goffman's (1974, p. 10) particularly apt term. Your task is to frame or make sense of these uninterpreted materials with a view to writing a sociohistorical account. The preceding chapter outlined three strategies for organizing archival data, and in this chapter we review several methodological complexities that can complicate the deceptively straightforward process of constructing chronologies, networks, and backstage dramas. The complexities include: (a) the seductive concreteness of tertiary sedimentations, (b) the failure to discern multiple communication channels, (c) the instability of "truth" in iterative research, (d) bracketing the perspective of the present to understand the past, and (e) the structural vulnerability of knowledge to intentional fabrication.

Getting Caught in the Concrete

Methodologically, we must always remain open to alternative ways to make sense of the physical traces that reside in archives. If the materials and the organizational structures established by archivists during tertiary sedimentation are taken for granted (Schutz, 1970-1971), researchers risk misinterpreting the archival evidence. The concreteness of the order imposed by the archivist's labels, chronologies, and file folders is directly experienced when materials are made available to researchers on a box-by-box basis. It is tempting to take this immediate experience and imposed order for granted—because they are something real in themselves—but they may blind us to the sociohistorical reality we intend to excavate. Each researcher must consciously ask: (a) How might the archival "strip" be otherwise organized for my purposes? (b) what is missing? (c) what multiple channels of communication exist within the sedimented archival record? and (d) am I the victim of a fabrication?

Goffman's (1974) frame analytic perspective orients the discussion. The strip is a foundational concept in Goffman's (1974) analysis of meaning:

> The term "strip" will be used to refer to any arbitrary slice or cut from the stream of ongoing activity, including here sequences of happenings, real or fictive, as seen from the perspective of those subjectively involved in sustaining an interest in them. A strip is not meant to reflect a natural division made by the subjects of inquiry or an analytical division made by students who inquire; *it will be used only to refer to any raw batch of occurrences* (of whatever status in reality) *that one wants to draw attention to as a starting point for analysis* [emphasis added]. (p. 10)

Strips comprise the raw, unorganized occurrences to which socialized adults quickly and routinely apply organization and meaning.

Sociohistorical researchers confront a "raw batch of occurrences" when they encounter archival materials face-to-file folder. Clearly, the contents of archives have already been shaped and framed by others during the major phases of sedimentation (Chapter 2). But the focus is now on how you respond: How do you decide to make order out of what you encounter in an archival file folder? By thinking of archival materials as unorganized strips, you purposefully free the material to be reorganized for your sociohistorical purposes. By consciously thinking of the archival record as a strip, we forcefully remind ourselves that the tertiary, secondary, and primary ordering of the materials during archival sedimentation may be at cross-purposes to our sociohistorical questions. The internal frame markers of tertiary archival organization (i.e., collections, boxes, files, chronology, alphabetization) need to be actively conceptualized as arbitrary anchors of sedimentary organization rather than unreflexively disattended.

How can we conceptually rearrange archival records to better suit our purposes? There are numerous possibilities, limited primarily by tradition and lack of imagination. The running dialogue between two correspondents, for example, may come into sharper relief and gain new significance when abstracted from the chronological record as a whole. Topical rather than temporal organization of materials is often helpful, for example, to consider as a whole all documents that address the topics of ecology, personality, or operationalism. Various types of documents can be cross-classified by structural characteristics. For example, letters of reference, sorted by size of college or university to which they were sent, might inform us about hierarchical patterns of bias in educational organizations. We can play hypothetically with the categories that archivists assign to materials. For example, what are the consequences for intellectual history if the yellowing leaves filed by an archivist as lecture notes are really the draft pages of an unfinished, unpublished book manuscript?

Conceptualizing archival holdings as uninterpreted strips reminds us that archival collections are necessarily partial in character. Noting what is not in the collection may be as important as knowing what survived. Absence of materials does not mean that they or their authors are unimportant. Conversely, the concrete survival of an item does not mean it is significant. In using archival data to piece together an historical scenario, we ask not only "What does this item tell us?" but also, "Why is this item here? Why did it survive and not something else?" and "What is missing?"

Multiple Communications

Archival items vary structurally in their communicative complexity.[1] Communication media often carry more channels of information than they officially advertise. Written communications (using such devices as code words and inside jokes) may contain "concealment channels" that the uninitiated reader may not recognize (Goffman, 1974, pp. 210-223). Indeed, an author inadvertently (or purposefully!) might carry concealment to an extreme, such that letters never sent to their intended recipients reside now in an archive to be misframed by us as communications.

Written media can also have "overlay channels" conveying two or more sequences of communication, possibly written at different times. For example, Edward A. Ross frequently made lists of "things to do" on the backs of letters he received. Archivally, the letters are chronologically arranged and indexed by correspondents' names. Ross's overlay channel, however, carries quite different data—sometimes of a domestic nature, sometimes plans for hunting trips, and so forth—that were disattended and thus not indexed by the archival organizers of the Ross papers. In other cases, organizational letterheads frequently carry data about the organization's officers, committee structures, and membership networks that are totally independent of the letter writer's main agenda. Additional examples of multiple channels include marginal notes made in books, instructor's comments on examination papers, "tick marks" indicating possible choices in book catalogs, and doodles beside frequently called numbers in a telephone book. Overlay notes penned in the margins of letters may not be marks made by your target, but by a biographer who used the letters prior to their transmittal to the archive.

Knowledge and Iteration

Archival work is iterative and continuing. Researchers revisit archives to reread materials, and visit new archives to expand their data base. We may see something new in a document already carefully considered many times before and, perhaps, dismissed earlier as irrelevant. Rereading collections is an important operation in archival research. This process is enormously facilitated today by microforms and photocopies. We can often reread and rearrange archival materials at our leisure, and at minimal expense. Iterative rereading suggests alternative organizations of the archival record and this, in turn, frequently results in the integral connection of once seemingly disparate data.

The potential to read and reread archival data with the benefit of hindsight and widening understanding places the archival researcher in a radically different relation to events than that experienced by historical participants at the time. For example, we read Edward A. Ross's 1899 Christmas letter to his adopted mother telling of his happy satisfaction with Stanford University knowing that Ross will be fired in 1900 and become the center of a national free-speech controversy.[2] We read Roscoe Pound's youthful self-estimate that he will become a "pretty fair lawyer," knowing that he will later be Dean of the Harvard University Law School.[3] The perspective of the present can tempt us to frame the past as irony, but sociohistorical patterns are much more than irony or idiosyncratic anecdotes. Sociohistory and intellectual biography are, rather, attempts to understand organizational processes and institutional forces as they unfold across time and space.

In discovering new materials through ongoing archival research, we are likely to uncover data that alter our prior understanding of our target and the social situation in which he or she worked and lived. The density of your data base increases as you visit more and more archives. When both sides of a series of letters between two writers are finally obtained, the one side previously known changes, sometimes dramatically. Third party commentaries may be discovered, and the meaning of the letters may change yet again. We may eventually see that an author wrote one version of events to one correspondent, and different accounts to others. New data are continually made sense of comprehensively, with reference to the entire record so far discovered—not just mechanically pigeonholed in spatiotemporal chronologies. The iterative process is cumulative but never absolute nor complete. Researchers continually reshape their understanding of the past as they fit, sort, shift, and reinterpret more and more data into evolving sociohistorical frameworks—guided by theory and creative sparks of insight.

Strangers to the Past

Archival researchers share much in common with strangers who visit and learn about new societies and life-worlds. As Schutz put it, the stranger "becomes essentially the man who has to place in question nearly everything that seems to be unquestionable to the members of the approached group" (1970-1971, Vol. II, p. 96). It is a phenomenological paradox that to understand the organization, rules, and conventions of past social groups, it is necessary to understand them consciously whereas the historical participants simply took those patterns and conventions for granted. Alternatively (and unforgivably), researchers too often project modern meanings onto the historical record and thereby jettison the phenomenological dictum to "bracket" our presuppositions (Schutz, 1970-1971, Vol. I, pp. 104-106).

The stranger in Schutz's strange land, unlike the archival researcher, is embedded in a series of ongoing social interactions. These situations permit the stranger immediate opportunities to test his or her mastery of local customs in situ, aided by authoritative residents who can correct mistakes. As archival researchers, on the other hand, we "visit" the past vicariously, discern patterns in archival traces, and return home to the present to publish our findings. Our reality check occurs in our home era rather than in the place and time from which our data are radically abstracted. We can understand the archival past, but never as the participants experienced it in the "natural attitude" (Schutz & Luckmann, 1973, pp. 3-20). However, in terms of the social scientific task of making rules, conventions, and organization explicit, we may better understand "history" than did the participants we study.

Fabrication and Vulnerability

Finally, as researchers, we must live existentially with the real possibility that our understanding of the past is at best presumptuous. The core message that Goffman (1974) teaches is that all knowledge is vulnerable to fabrication—and may at any time crumble like a house of cards. There is always the possibility that posterity is being "contained" or duped by our sociohistorical targets or some other active agent of disinformation during the process of archival sedimentation. Perhaps our target planted fabricated materials in his or her archival legacy as a personal revenge or a private joke! Containment can be benign (wherein researchers are merely the butt of a target's practical jest) or exploitative (in which investigators are purposefully misled, for example, into discrediting a target's former enemies). Both possibilities, if realized, would seriously distort our sociohistorical accounts and make a travesty of scholarship—it is tempting to discount their likelihood. The possibilities, however, reflect the built-in, structural vulnerabilities of human knowledge that Goffman so astutely understood.

The search for social scientific understanding of past events is a methodologically complex framing problem replete with traps and detours. This search requires reflexivity, openness to alternative interpretations, attention to multiple data sources, and peripatetic investigation in archives across the country, if not the world. Our iterative, reflexive framing of intersubjectively verifiable archival data lies at the heart of this project. Received dogmas are fundamentally inimical to archival analysis. Findings in the field of sociohistorical investigation are always tentative and subject to constant reinterpretation; it is not a project for researchers who seek unchallenged truths.

NOTES

1. Goffman (1974, pp. 201-246) discusses these issues in terms of what he calls "out-of-frame activity."
2. Ross to his mother, 15 December 1899, Box 2, Folder 2, Edward A. Ross Papers, State Historical Society of Wisconsin, Madison, Wisconsin.
3. Pound to Hershey, 14 August 1892, Paul Sayre Papers, University Archive, University of Iowa, Iowa City, Iowa.

10. PUBLICATION, CITATIONS, AND PERMISSIONS

The publication of materials gleaned from archival repositories involves somewhat more than simply inserting appropriate quotations and footnotes in your manuscript. Typically, you must obtain permission to publish even short quotations or extracts of unpublished materials from archival repositories.[1] In the best of cases, the repository controls the publication rights and directly gives you permission to publish. In more complicated situations, you may need to obtain not only the permission of the archive, but also the consent of the copyright owner. The latter may be the author of a letter you want to quote, the executor of the author's estate, the author's surviving relatives, and so on. It is useful to remember that unless otherwise assigned, copyright resides with the author (not the recipient) of any unpublished material, including personal letters. For further discussion of copyright issues, see Strong (1990).

The problem of permissions can mushroom exponentially. For example, suppose you write an article in which you document your target's life by quoting directly from several letters sent to your target, and these letters were written by (for the sake of an example) 30 different correspondents (some deceased and some still living). Legally, you may be obligated to make a "best effort" attempt to contact each author or surviving relative/executor and obtain written permission to publish. Some archives may be able to provide you with names and addresses of those whose permissions you need, but often you are on your own to identify and track down the proper parties. In any event, ask questions about copyright when you visit each archive. It may be particularly advisable to seek advice from an attorney if your case becomes complicated, involves publishing material that might be considered libelous, or runs the happy risk of becoming a runaway hit on *The New York Times* best-seller list.

Some authors, relatives, or executors may refuse permission for a variety of reasons, thus taxing your diplomatic skills to the limit. The copyright owner may be functionally senile and closeted in a nursing home, or may wrongly suspect you of trying to make a fortune by publishing a loved one's letters. Family members may want "that old scandal" hushed up and left "best forgotten." Regardless of your legal obligations, it is a matter of common courtesy to contact family members and advise them of your interests and the nature of your research project.

A variety of situations can ameliorate the difficulty of obtaining permissions. If you choose to write about a subject who died many years ago, the permissions problem can actually improve. Once an author's grandchildren die, the copyright may in some circumstances pass to the public domain. Matters may be greatly simplified if the author of a quoted letter had no siblings, never married, and had no offspring (and this situation is not so unusual as might be supposed). Copyright to letters in government archives and administrative correspondence in the archives of public institutions such as state universities usually resides in the public domain, or this material may be publishable under the Freedom of Information Act.

If permissions are denied or unattainable, all is not lost. Typically, you will successfully obtain at least some portion of the needed permissions. Remember, too, that you have been seeking permissions to publish verbatim quotations. You are off the hook if you are willing to settle for paraphrases. If you cannot provide a quotation as direct evidence of a certain point, you can at least tell your readers exactly where to find the relevant document(s) in an archive so they can read your source for themselves.

One of the curious charms of archival research is the ability to make unassailable claims to intersubjective verifiability. By carefully citing every archival document from which you quote or to which you make reference, you open your research to the kind of double-checking required by the most stringent rules of scientific investigation. Furthermore, careful citation of your documentary evidence makes your research cumulative in a particularly useful sense. By reading your work, scholars with related interests learn of archival collections and specific unpublished materials that may save them months or years of unproductive searching. The materials you find may allow another scholar to frame a radically new interpretation of his or her own archival discoveries. Indeed, your work may someday be the focus of someone else's literature review.

The public character of archival data also warrants a caution. Significant archival discoveries typically represent an enormous investment in time, money, sweat, and archival acumen—and thus it may be wise to keep your discoveries "close to the vest" until you see them safely into print. Remember, too, that so-called blind reviewers of manuscripts submitted for publication get to see your citations and documentation months and perhaps years before your work is published. The review process is, unfortunately, a situation ripe for unscrupulous exploitation.

Unethical reviewers aside, the more precisely you can identify the exact location of a cited document, the better it is for all concerned. Documentation of archival data, quotations, and references is usually placed in sequentially numbered footnotes that provide:

1. the names of the correspondents (if a letter) or a short, identifying description of the document (such as the title of a manuscript or a descriptor such as "memo," "Johnson's diary," "Sociology 101 lecture notes," etc.);
2. the date of the document, if known;

3. the exact box number;
4. the exact folder number (or folder title);
5. the name of the collection;
6. the name of the archive; and
7. the university, or city and state, where the archive is located.

Consider the following hypothetical models suggested by archivists:

1. Letter, Smith to Roberts, 5 Aug 1907, Box 62, folder 3, John Breslow Roberts Collection, Bradshaw University Archives.
2. Memo, unsigned, 25 Jan 1923, Box 2, folder "memos and telegrams," Edward J. Rossiter Papers, Cleveland State Historical Society, Oxford, Ohio.
3. "Scientific Theories," p. 7, unpublished paper by T. R. Smith, undated, Box 52, folder "unpublished manuscripts," Roberta Mason Smith Papers, Tractor State University Archives, Des Moines, Iowa.

The format and conventions you finally adopt depend in part on your own sense of bibliographic style, your publisher's requirements (these typically follow the *Chicago Manual of Style*), and the requirements set by particular archives.

When your manuscript is ready for publication, write to each archive and copyright holder to secure permission to publish each quotation or extract. In your request, provide photocopies of (a) each quotation and its context in your work, and (b) each documentary footnote that identifies the source of the quotation. The rare archivist may question your interpretation of a piece of evidence, but most archivists are interested primarily in making sure that your documentation is correct. Documentation errors may cause headaches not only for other researchers but also for the archivist in question. Be sure to keep copies of all permissions you receive. When your work is accepted for publication, your publisher may want to see copies of permissions before your manuscript is finally placed in production.

Prior to publication, it is good practice to solicit the input of all informants, if any, who may have contributed to your study. It may be useful to have a few scholars who specialize in the history of your target review your manuscript for errors and suggest revisions. Finally, remember that all research is a collective, socially embedded enterprise. Be sure to include an acknowledgment in your manuscript thanking everyone who helped you, including archivists, archival staff, librarians, informants, reviewers, and so on. It is surprising how long the list can become! When finally published, it is common courtesy (and good public relations) to send copies of your work to those who made your publication possible, including archives, informants, and the friends, family, and colleagues of sociohistorical targets who shared their time and information with you.

NOTES

1. More often than not, researchers are required to sign a form acknowledging this requirement during the orientation interview. For discussions by archivists on copyrights, see Porter (1981), Crawford (1983), and Post (1983).

11. NONARCHIVAL DATA SOURCES

Sociohistorical researchers make use of relevant data from many sources, published and unpublished, archival and nonarchival. Any number of nonarchival data sources can compensate or complement when relevant materials in formal archives are unavailable, are fragmentary, or require triangulation and corroboration. The vagaries by which materials are deposited in archives are unpredictable, causing "holes" even in comprehensive archival collections. Alternative data sources can help bridge the gap when formal archival deposits are incomplete or missing.

The range and variety of useful alternative data sources are constrained primarily by your imagination and resourcefulness. The extraordinary variability of materials found in archival collections gives a hint to the myriad places in which you might also look for data outside of formal archives per se, perhaps in a library, a museum director's office, or the files of a private collector.[1] For example, a scrapbook of pertinent newspaper clippings found in an archival collection suggests going directly to microfilm copies of relevant newspapers in local public libraries to search for additional data or to supplement the record when an archival collection does not contain such a scrapbook.

Numerous nonarchival data facilities are maintained by public, private, and quasi-public organizations. Surprisingly individualized detail is collected and maintained by a welter of private and quasi-public organizations, such as credit bureaus, compilers of city directories, insurance

companies, hospitals, schools, professional associations, fraternal societies, and alumni associations (Neier, 1975; Rule, 1974). All such sources
have potential uses, depending on the questions you want to ask. For example, turn-of-the-century city directories can be used to discover the home
addresses of university professors. The addresses can then be plotted on city
maps to reconstruct the residential relationships of university scholars.

Many U.S. government records are found in the U.S. National Archives
and Records Administration (Davis, 1988), but others, ostensibly for
reasons of secrecy and confidentiality, are separately maintained by agencies but may be accessible via the Freedom of Information Act (Adler,
1990; U.S. Congress, 1977). Mike Keen (1991), for example, recently
obtained the FBI files of several prominent sociologists, thus documenting official government interest in the ideological positions professed by
American social scientists. Buitrago and Immerman (1981) provide a
detailed guide to excavating your own FBI files, and thus to retrieving the
files of others. When requesting FBI files other than your own, you must
provide documentary evidence that the person whose file you seek has
died (a photocopy of an obituary from a newspaper will usually suffice).
Hourly charges for locating FBI materials can be waived if you document
your status as a qualified scholar working on a scholarly project, but you
will be obligated to pay all photocopy charges.

State and local records that are regularly searched by genealogists
(Eakle & Cerny, 1984; Stevenson, 1977) may have use in any given study.
Court records and trial transcripts, voter registrations, birth certificates,
and property tax assessments represent only the tip of enormous, public
repositories of sociohistorically useful information. Local newspapers are
gold mines of spatiotemporal data.

Privately held materials can also be very useful. A large number of letters,
manuscripts, and memorabilia of famous personages (noted writers and
major intellectuals, included) have been assembled by private collectors,
often at considerable expense.[2] Of greater potential use, however, are
materials that are presently collecting dust (if not mildew) in the attics and
basements of your target's relatives. Locating these nonarchival deposits
may be as simple as writing to surviving relatives or placing advertise-
ments (briefly describing your study and requesting information about your
target) in appropriate newspapers, association publications, and alumni
newsletters. In addition to discovering actual documents per se, you may
happily chance to locate a relative, former co-worker, or student who has

vivid memories of your target and can provide you with firsthand data and descriptions that you could recover in no other way. In sum, discovering and gaining access to private and quasi-public materials typically requires patience, diplomacy, and a bureaucratically astute imagination.

The sociohistorical uses of nonarchival data are limitless. Scholarly and analytical exploitation depends only on your creativity and resourcefulness. The didactic examples presented below illustrate only two of myriad ways in which to capitalize on alternate data sources.

Example 1: Reconstructed Libraries

The assumption here is that you want to identify the published intellectual sources your target consulted as a young scholar, perhaps like yourself. If you do not have a set of letters in which your target discussed which books he or she read as a student, you may still be able to locate other evidence of the subject's bibliographic interests. An obvious approach is to look at footnotes in your target's publications and identify materials that were contemporaneous with your target's schooling—perhaps those subsequently cited books were your target's assigned readings in a college course.

You can also search for other physical traces as well. For example, you can sometimes note the use by your target of particular library books by examining the signatures on library charge cards (an opportunity that is fast disappearing as libraries shift to computer-based charge systems). Or you might use the knowledge that your target enrolled in a specific college course (information gleaned from your target's college transcript) combined with the reading list of assigned authors in the course (data retrieved from a college bulletin for the appropriate year) to deduce what books your target's instructor intended him or her to read.

Better yet, your target may have preserved his or her personal book collection or may have donated it intact to a library. A few scholars, Roscoe Pound, for example, maintained their personal libraries intact, and these can be physically searched for relevant titles, inscriptions, marginal notes, indications of year of purchase, and so forth (Hill, 1989e). Other scholars donated their libraries to universities, and these can sometimes be traced by searching for donors' bookplates or "GIFT OF _____" notations. Hutton Webster, the first American professor of social anthropology, donated his books to Stanford University where they were later

integrated with other collections. Webster's library can be partially reconstructed, however, by systematically searching for bookplates in the
folklore section of the Stanford library.

It also pays to be alert at secondhand book stores and used book sales.
Edith Abbott, an early sociologist at the University of Chicago and a
Nebraska native (Costin, 1983; Deegan, 1979; Deegan & Hill, 1991b),
donated her library to the University of Nebraska in the 1950s. Years later,
the university library declared many of the volumes "duplicates" and sold
them at a book sale. Fortunately, hundreds of the books were rounded up
(including dozens of volumes that were shipped to a local secondhand
thrift store) and donated to the University of Illinois at Chicago where
they reside together once again as the Edith Abbott Bluestem Collection
(Deegan & Hill, 1988).[3] All such physical traces—bookplates, inscriptions, even whole libraries—can be used as supporting evidence of a
scholar's reading habits, or at least book-collecting predilections.

Another tack would be to ask, "What books were available to your
subject at a given place and time in his or her intellectual career?" You
might try locating a copy of a library's printed catalog from your target's
hometown. For example, the small town of Coldwater, Michigan, published its library's catalog, thus documenting the volumes available to
young people, including Frances Kellor (Deegan, 1991, pp. 209-216),
who grew up in that midwestern village in the late 19th century. The John
Crerar Library (1909) similarly published a list of "the books kept on open
shelves in the General Reading Room, which are used by the public
without any formality," thus documenting works available in the library's
Chicago neighborhood at the turn of the century.[4]

Another way to identify books that your target might have known about
as a youngster is to examine local newspapers of the era. Newspapers sometimes announced the arrival of "new titles" acquired by public libraries.
Books advertised or reviewed in local papers and popular magazines are
evidence of books that were "in the air" and about which your target might
well have had at least a passing acquaintance. The point of all this is that
there are many ways to address the question, "What books did your target
read?" using a host of published and/or nonarchival evidentiary sources.

Example 2: Public Speaking Engagements

In this second example, assume that you want to reconstruct the pattern
of your target's public speeches. We ask ourselves: "Where would announce-

ments and reports or reviews of those public speeches have appeared?" The likely answers are handbills, programs, newspapers, newsletters of sympathetic or sponsoring organizations, thank-you letters sent to the speaker, annual reports, club minutes, and so forth. Note that such items are frequently found in archive deposits, but it may not be sufficient to look at archives only.

Many archival collections include scrapbooks of newspaper clippings, files of programs, letters from appreciative fans, and so on. At the same time, the official minutes of an ongoing social club that once hosted your target as a speaker may still be in the possession of the club's current secretary or club historian. Oral interviews are often found in archives,[5] but the interviews you need might still need to be conducted with living subjects. The fact that you set out to do archival work does not preclude conducting interviews when necessary. Traditional library research may be required to track down microfilms of relevant newspapers or back issues of a club magazine (such as the *City Club Bulletin* of Chicago, for example). The only way to obtain old issues of a fraternity's alumni newsletter may be to contact the fraternity's elder members. In short, the moral is that when the archival record is missing or incomplete, you can often fill the breach by resourcefully turning to a variety of nonarchival data sources.

Summary

The use and relevance of nonarchival sources depend on the specific situation, availability, and the questions researchers want to answer. Most important, nonarchival trace evidence can fill gaps in the archival record. The potentially nonreactive character of alternative trace data (Webb, Campbell, Schwartz, & Sechrest, 1966) can sometimes corroborate or discredit information found in archival deposits. For example, if your target claimed in a letter to have grown up in a ramshackle house, you may be able to check local tax records to verify the valuation of the family home at the time of the target's birth.

In truth, the distinction between archival and nonarchival materials is often pragmatic rather than substantive. In any given case, an archival collection may or may not contain any or all of the types of materials discussed in this chapter (i.e., newspapers, organizational minutes, personal libraries, credit reports, transcripts, bank records, income tax returns, confidential files, and so on). If the data in such materials are useful to your project, then it behooves you to track them down wherever they repose, inside or outside of formal archives.

NOTES

1. As an example, note Lela Costin's out-of-the-way discovery of material for her study of Grace and Edith Abbott: "The Annual Reports of St. Hilda's Settlement can hardly be said to reside in a manuscript collection, but they did supply essential information to understanding Edith Abbott's residence in that settlement and her work in its neighborhood. St. Hilda's today is very different than in 1906. My visit to the settlement in behalf of my study aroused the curiosity of the young director and he allowed me to search in a cupboard at the settlement where, amidst an array of diverse materials, copies of the old annual reports were unearthed" (Costin, 1983, pp. 242).

2. I was delighted—and my bank account subsequently depleted—when a rare book dealer called recently and offered me the opportunity to purchase a letter in which Harriet Martineau, one of the earliest sociologists, briefly discussed her plan to translate Comte's *Positive Philosophy* into English.

3. Book dealers Pat and Scott Wendt of Bluestem Books, Lincoln, Nebraska, played a central role in salvaging this major scholarly collection.

4. The library was subsequently removed to the campus of the University of Chicago, where it remains today.

5. Indeed, useful oral interviews with your target or people who knew your target may already be available. Be sure to check if the interviews in the Columbia University Oral History Project are available at your local library.

APPENDIX

Epistemology and the Search for Unsung Social Scientists: A Rationale and Pragmatic Strategies

The recovery of unknown or presently discounted social scientists is an important epistemological task to which archival research can make significant contributions. This appendix outlines a rationale for taking epistemological concerns with you to the archives and enumerates several "habits of mind" that will help you uncover theorists, concepts, and empirical discoveries on which to build forward-looking alternative visions of the social sciences. Readers are cautioned, however, that searching for unknown but otherwise insightful social scientists typically requires patience and a long-term approach to archival research.

In hegemonic intellectual systems such as the discipline-based, departmentally structured social sciences, disregarded or little-known scholars are not ipso facto worthless, unproductive, or uninteresting. Rather, their ideas are simply not cited, read, or reproduced. Evaluation of their actual and potential intellectual import for modern social theory and practice is quite a separate matter, and one for which we are all more rather than less responsible. Recovery efforts are especially important in reference to the roles of women and people of color in the origins and development of sociology (Deegan, 1991).

Retrieving hegemonically oppressed ideas and theories helps us avoid continually reinventing the wheel. It is shocking how many books of the past two decades claim to address a topic for the first time when, in fact, the issues were confronted comprehensively in prior eras by social scientists who evidenced greater insight, humanity, and sophistication. Reinhartz (1992), for example, does an extraordinary service in excavating the historical roots of feminist methodology. Deegan (1992) shows how settlement-based sociologists in turn-of-the-century Chicago learned much about immigrants and ethnic diversity that is applicable in Europe today. What other insights do long-forgotten social scientists have to tell us about our social institutions? Archival research is not just a window on the past; it also helps us see our present methodological quandaries and social problems from thoughtful, constructive, and proven prospectives.

As theorists, we ought to ask, "What if?" What if a perceptive but now ignored social scientist had become the "theorist of choice" in a hegemonically dominant school of social science? What would that discipline look like today? Based on a scholar's work and using inferential logic, that alternative social science discipline can be reconstructed. Asking "What if?" as social science theorists is not like asking "What if?" as historians. As theorists, we can reconstruct alternative social sciences based on the archival recovery and intellectual evaluation of theories discounted and undervalued by hegemonic factions within our disciplines. These recovered intellectual systems, when fully articulated, become alternative intellectual antecedents for the social sciences today and in the future. This, ultimately, is a significant promise and hope of sociohistorically grounded archival research in the history of the social sciences.

Archival files are also filled with data that can, if we look for them, reveal the inner workings of social and organizational processes that shape the content and character of the social sciences. We can learn how schools of thought are constructed; how a few people become insiders while others, just as gifted, are relegated to lives as disenfranchised outsiders. We can explicate the ways in which professional reputations are constructed, deconstructed, and reconstructed, and how some topics become "hot" while others never flirt with the flames of fashion.

There are many projects that require archival exploration. For example, we need to better understand the history and impact on the social sciences of loyalty oaths and the McCarthy era; of racially and sexually segregated professional organizations;

of internal power struggles in disciplinary cliques; of foundations, government agencies, and the politics of social science research funding; and of the dynamics of sexual harassment and homophobia. These vital topics can be subjects of archival research. Understanding these events and processes can give us the insight needed to revolutionize the social sciences as organizational projects.[1]

Perhaps the most important roadblocks to recovering unknown social scientists and their work are perversely conceptual. Insecurities about professional identities combined with 20th-century turf battles between the social sciences—and with the humanities—have resulted in gate-keeping definitions of specific disciplines that are, to put it bluntly: petty, mean-spirited, vindictive, self-serving, and frequently racist and/or sexist. If you join the search for unrecognized contributors to the social sciences, prepare yourself for a barrage of ill-founded advice that your project has no relevance, theoretical or otherwise, to modern social science disciplines.[2]

The archival practices that make name-oriented search strategies (Chapter 4) productive are, in fact, part of the mechanism that drives the social construction of fame versus obscurity. It is much easier to do archival projects about well-known people. Their materials are more highly treasured, more likely to be deposited in archival collections, and more apt to be carefully inventoried and cataloged. The famous are, by definition, more often found in biographical dictionaries and in literature searches.

Although there is still much to clarify in the intellectual biographies of institutionally prominent, oft-cited social scientists, it is pertinent to ask seriously: Do we need more look-alike monographs on Durkheim, Weber, or Marx[3] when there are other social scientists, such as Harriet Martineau, Charlotte Perkins Gilman, or Irene Diggs, about whom we know relatively little? Must we add more volumes to the scores of histories on the Chicago school,[4] for example, when so many other sociology departments remain unchronicled by even a single article, let alone a monograph? Whatever else it does, archival research opens opportunities for you to move beyond the standard treatments toward original work that is fresh, reflexive, and inclusionary.

Long-term archival research is a proven mechanism for tapping into intellectual activity and the collegial networks of social scientists who are not easily traced in standard literature searches. The suggestions in this appendix are specifically for researchers who want to unearth the stories of the unsung or the presently obscure—the hard-to-find needles in archival haystacks. Pragmatically, the most productive process for discovering unrecognized intellectual and organizational contributions to the various social sciences is to piggyback your long-term agenda on a series of shorter-term and more sharply defined projects. You are most likely to stumble across archival traces of lesser known social scientists as secondary sedimentations in the collections of institutionally more established scholars (Chapter 2). Gloria Urch (1992) recounts discovering Rachel Harris, reportedly the only Afro-American nurse from the U.S. Civil War era, while searching for something quite different:

> I was looking for something else when I found her photo in a file at the county historical society. I held it for a moment and studied it . . . . I put her photo aside and continued my research. A few minutes later, the photo—which I thought I had placed securely on the shelf above me—fell into my lap, and those same eyes were gazing up into mine again. Before I left that day I made a copy of Rachel's photo and obituary and tucked it away. (p. 8)

Thus began Urch's inquiry into the life and times of Rachel Harris. The point is that you never know when you will encounter a person or event that piques your interest. One key is to read and study the archival records of disciplinary leaders while purposefully keeping an eye open for materials that identify and illuminate the lives and work of the unknown and the unrecognized.

As you work on your principal enterprise, consider building a separate file in which you collect information about social scientists who inhabit the margins of your current project. You will collect many useful leads, data, and ideas if you systematically cultivate the following habits:

1. When reading archival collections, be alert for materials or references relating to persons of minority status, specifically: women, persons of color, and members of oppressed minorities generally. I know one researcher who photocopies every letter she finds that is written to or by a woman regardless of how tangential the letters seem at the moment.
2. Search for and examine carefully the work of scholars in schools outside the currently acknowledged "prestige" academies. For example, be particularly alert for non-Chicago and non-Columbia sociologists and their collegial networks.
3. Be alert to professional achievements outside the academy; for example, in business, philanthropy, or government.
4. Remember that professional training in a discipline other than your own does not negate the potential import of a scholar's work for your own disciplinary history or future intellectual development.
5. Look for instances of mentoring through patterns other than formal student-teacher relationships (for example, apprenticeship to a statistician in a municipal information bureau, or becoming the proofreader or managing editor of a social science journal).
6. Do not be immediately dissuaded by claims to (or attributions of) professional identities other than your discipline of focus (Deegan, 1987a).
7. Consider the possibility that a scholar may have multiple professional identities in two or more disciplines.
8. Remember, evidence that scholars did not closely identify with a particular discipline at a particular time does not mean that they did not so identify themselves at some other time in their careers.

9. Advocacy of views unpopular among or critical of the dominant disciplinary perspectives may signal the work of a scholar who was hegemonically suppressed. Be especially attentive to the possibility of unpublished monographs, rejected journal articles, and articles clipped from local newspapers or small-circulation publications that could easily be missed in even the widest state-of-the-art literature search.

10. Be alert to behind-the-scenes organizational and administrative "shadow work" (Illich, 1982) that facilitates teaching, research, and publication by others. This includes such tasks as collecting data, teaching extension and night courses, or doing organizational work "backstage."

11. The fact that a school or university had no formally organized academic department for any given social science discipline does not mean that disciplinary activity was absent.

The suggestions in this appendix, if patiently and systematically applied, are the framework for the long-term archival rediscovery of our wider collective intellectual heritage and interdisciplinary relationships. Do not lose heart if you do not recover an unheralded social scientist during the course of your first archival project, however. The exclusionary consequences of decades of structural inequity and hegemony in the social sciences are not easily or quickly recovered or repaired.

NOTES

1. When they are unsealed in the coming years, the files of the ASA Committee on Freedom in Research and Teaching (COFRAT), now housed among the Papers of the American Sociological Association at the Library of Congress, will provide many insights into these topics.

2. There seem to be any number of so-called authorities who are more than willing to pontificate unreflexively about who is and who is not a member of the elect in any given social scientific discipline. For objective criteria to use in rebuttal, see Deegan's (1988a) adaptation of Kasler's (1981) yardsticks for identifying sociologists in Germany.

3. The scholarship radiating from these figures is overwhelming. For example, Nandan (1977) lists more than 7,000 Durkheimian studies alone.

4. Kurtz (1984) lists over 1,000 studies concerned with various aspects of the Chicago school of sociology.

REFERENCES

Abbott, E. (1939). Grace Abbott: A sister's memories. *Social Service Review, 13*(3), 351-407.

Abbott. E. (1950). Grace Abbott and Hull House, 1908-1921. *Social Service Review, 24*(3), 374-394; (4), 493-518.

Addams, J. (1916). *The long road of woman's memory*. New York: Macmillan.

Adler, A. R. (1990). *Using the Freedom of Information Act: A step by step guide*. Washington, DC: American Civil Liberties Union.

Altham, E., Godfrey, J. E., Mahan, R. E., & Rice, R. H. (Eds.). (1988). *Index to personal names in the national union catalog of manuscript collections, 1959-1984*. Alexandria, VA: Chadwyck-Healey.

Balander, G. (1974). *Gurvitch*. Explorations in Interpretive Sociology series. New York: Harper & Row.

Bart, P., & Frankel, L. (1981). *The student sociologist's handbook*. Glenview, IL: Scott, Foresman.

Berger, P. L., & Luckmann, T. (1966). *The social construction of reality*. Garden City, NY: Doubleday.

Blackwell, J., & Janowitz, M. (Eds.). (1974). *Black sociologists: Historical and contemporary perspectives* [Heritage of Sociology series]. Chicago: University of Chicago Press.

Blalock, H. M. (1972). *Social statistics* (2nd ed.). New York: McGraw-Hill.

Bok, S. (1978). *Lying: Moral choice in public and private life*. New York: Pantheon.

Brichford, M. (1980). Academic Archives: *Uberlieferungsbildung* [Cultural transfer]. *American Archivist, 43*(4), 449-460.

Brooks, P. C. (1969). *Research in archives: The use of unpublished primary sources*. Chicago: University of Chicago Press.

Buitrago, A. M., & Immerman, L. A. (1981). *Are you now or have you ever been in the FBI files?: How to secure and interpret your FBI files*. New York: Grove.

Burke, F. G. (1981). The future course of archival theory in the United States. *American Archivist, 44*(1), 40-46.

Conway, P. (1986). Facts and frameworks: An approach to studying the users of archives. *American Archivist, 49*(4), 393-407.

Costin, L. B. (1983). *Two sisters for social justice: A biography of Grace and Edith Abbott*. Urbana: University of Illinois Press.

Crawford, M. J. (1983). Copyright, unpublished manuscript records, and the archivist. *American Archivist, 46*(2), 135-147.

Cushing, H. G., & Morris, A. V. (1944). *Nineteenth century readers' guide to periodical literature, 1890-1899; With supplementary indexing, 1900-1922* (2 vols.). New York: H. W. Wilson.

Davis, E. S. (Compiler). (1988). *Holdings list of U.S. National Archives and Records Administration*. Chicago: Center for Research Libraries.

Deegan, M. J. (1979). Edith Abbott. In L. Mainiero (Ed.), *American women writers* (Vol. I, pp. 3-5). New York: Frederick Ungar.

Deegan, M. J. (1981). Early women sociologists and the American Sociological Society: The patterns of exclusion and participation. *American Sociologist, 16* (February), pp. 14-24.

Deegan, M. J. (1987a). *Not a sociologist: The historical redefinition of early women, activists, and humanist sociologists* [Photocopy]. Keynote address, James B. McKee Symposium, Department of Sociology, Michigan State University.

Deegan, M. J. (1987b). Working hypotheses for women and social change. In M. J. Deegan & M. R. Hill (Eds.), *Women and symbolic interaction* (pp. 443-449). Boston: Allen & Unwin.

Deegan, M. J. (1988a). *Jane Addams and the men of the Chicago school, 1892-1918*. New Brunswick, NJ: Transaction Books.

Deegan, M. J. (1988b). Transcending a patriarchal past: Teaching the history of women in sociology. *Teaching Sociology, 16* (April), 141-150.

Deegan, M. J. (1989). *American ritual dramas: Social rules and cultural meanings* [Contributions in Sociology, no. 76]. Westport, CT: Greenwood.

Deegan, M. J. (1990). Review of *Myths of the Chicago school of sociology* by Lee Harvey. *British Journal of Sociology, 41* (December), 587-590.

Deegan, M. J. (Ed.). (1991). *Women in sociology: A bio-bibliographical sourcebook*. Westport, CT: Greenwood.

Deegan, M. J. (1992). The genesis of the international self: Working hypotheses emerging from the Chicago experience (1892-1918). In L. Tomasi (Ed.), *Non-European youth and the process of integration for a tolerant society* (pp. 339-533). Trento, Italy: Reverdito Edizioni.

Deegan, M. J., & Hill, M. R. (Eds.). (1987). *Women and symbolic interaction*. Boston: Allen & Unwin.

Deegan, M. J., & Hill, M. R. (1988). The Edith Abbott Bluestem Collection [Photocopy]. Unpublished paper and bibliographic inventory. Bluestem Collection, Jane Addams Memorial Collection, University Library, University of Illinois at Chicago.

Deegan, M. J., & Hill, M. R. (1991a). Doctoral dissertations as liminal journeys of the self. *Teaching Sociology, 19* (July), 322-332.

Deegan, M. J., & Hill, M. R. (1991b). Edith Abbott. In M. J. Deegan (Ed.), *Women in sociology: A bio-bibliographical sourcebook* (pp. 29-36). Westport, CT: Greenwood.

Deegan, M. J., & Hill, M. R. (1991c). Lucile Eaves. In M. J. Deegan (Ed.), *Women in sociology: A bio-bibliographical sourcebook* (pp. 140-147). Westport, CT: Greenwood.

Deegan, M. J., & Hill, M. R. (1991d). Alice S. Rossi. In M. J. Deegan (Ed.), *Women in sociology: A bio-bibliographical sourcebook* (pp. 342-349). Westport, CT: Greenwood.

Denzin, N. K. (1989). *Interpretive biography* [Qualitative Research Methods Series]. Newbury Park, CA: Sage.

Dewey, J. (1913). Play. In P. Monroe (Ed.), *A cyclopedia of education* (Vol. 4, pp. 725-727). New York: Macmillan.

DuBois, W. E. B. (1899). *The Philadelphia Negro: A social study* [With a special report on domestic service by Isabel Eaton]. Philadelphia: University of Pennsylvania. (Studies in Political Economy and Public Law, No. 14).

Duckett, K. W. (1975). *Modern manuscripts: A practical manual for their management, care, and use*. Nashville, TN: American Association for State and Local History.

Eakle, A., & Cerny, J. (Eds.). (1984). *The source: A guidebook of American genealogy*. Salt Lake City, UT: Ancestry.

Farber, E. I. (Ed.). (1980). *Combined retrospective index to book reviews in scholarly journals, 1886-1974*. Arlington, VA: Carrollton.

Farber, E. I. (1982). *Combined retrospective index to book reviews in humanities journals, 1802-1974*. Woodbridge, CT: Research Publications.

Foster, J., & Sheppard, J. (1982). *British archives: A guide to archive resources in the United Kingdom*. Detroit, MI: Gale Research.

Foucault, M. (1979). *Discipline and punish: The birth of the prison* (A. Sheridan, Trans.). New York: Vintage.

Gacs, U., Khan, A., McIntyre, J., & Weinberg, R. (Eds.). (1988). *Women anthropologists: A biographical dictionary*. Westport, CT: Greenwood.

Giddens, A. (1987). *Sociology: A brief but critical introduction* (2nd ed.). San Diego, CA: Harcourt Brace Jovanovich.

Goffman, E. (1959). *The presentation of self in everyday life*. Garden City, NY: Doubleday.

Goffman, E. (1967). *Interaction ritual: Essays on face-to-face behavior*. Garden City, NY: Anchor Books.

Goffman, E. (1974). *Frame analysis: An essay on the organization of experience*. New York: Harper & Row.

Goffman, E. (1981). *Forms of talk*. Philadelphia: University of Pennsylvania Press.

Griffen, L. J., & Quadagno, J. (1988). *Didactic seminar on historical sociology*. Presented at the annual meeting of the American Sociological Association, Atlanta, GA.

Hammond, P. E. (Ed.). (1964). *Sociologists at work: Essays in the craft of social research*. New York: Basic Books.

Harvey, L. (1987). *Myths of the Chicago school of sociology*. Aldershot, England: Avebury.

Hill, M. R. (1981). Positivism: A 'hidden' perspective in geography. In M. E. Harvey & B. P. Holly (Eds.), *Themes in geographic thought* (pp. 38-60). London: Croom Helm.

Hill, M. R. (1984). Epistemology, axiology, and ideology in sociology. *Mid-American Review of Sociology, 9*, 59-77.

Hill, M. R. (1988a). Research by bureaucracy: Hattie Plum Williams and the National Commission on Law Observance and Enforcement. *Mid-American Review of Sociology, 13*(2), 69-84.

Hill, M. R. (1988b). Roscoe Pound and the *Seminarium Botanicum* at the University of Nebraska, 1888-1889. *Transactions of the Nebraska Academy of Sciences, 16*, 185-190.

Hill, M. R. (Ed.). (1988c). The foundations of Nebraska sociology [Special issue]. *Mid-American Review of Sociology, 13*(2), 1-103.

Hill, M. R. (1989a). *The dramaturgy of archival research: A frame analysis of disciplinary reconstruction in sociology*. Paper presented at the meetings of the Association for Humanist Sociology, Washington, DC.

Hill, M. R. (1989b). Empiricism and reason in Harriet Martineau's sociology. In H. Martineau, *How to observe morals and manners* (sesquicentennial ed.) (pp. xv-lx). [Social Science Classics Series]. New Brunswick, NJ: Transaction Books. (Original work published 1838)

Hill, M. R. (1989c). Mari Sandoz' sociological imagination: *Capital City* as an ideal type. *Platte Valley Review, 17*(1), 102-122.

Hill, M. R. (1989d). *Roscoe Pound and American sociology: A study in archival frame analysis, sociobiography, and sociological jurisprudence*. Unpublished doctoral dissertation, University of Nebraska-Lincoln, Department of Sociology.

Hill, M. R. (1989e). Roscoe Pound's sociological library: The foundations of American sociological jurisprudence (Public Administration Series, no. P-2632). Monticello, IL: Vance Bibliographies.

Hill, M. R. (1990a). *The archival records of the American Sociological Association at the U.S. Library of Congress: An inventory and introduction* (Final report, ASA Problems of the Discipline Grant). Lincoln: University of Nebraska-Lincoln, Department of Sociology.

Hill, M. R. (1990b). *Excavating underappreciated sociologists: A survey of assumptions and strategies in archival research*. Paper presented at the meetings of the American Sociological Association, Washington, DC.

Hill, M. R. (1991). Harriet Martineau. In M. J. Deegan (Ed.), *Women in sociology: A bio-bibliographical sourcebook* (pp. 287-297). Westport, CT: Greenwood.

Hill, M. R. (1992). Eva Jeany Ross, Catholic sociologist, 1903-1969. *Midwest Feminist Papers, 2,* 5-7 [New series].

Hill, M. R. (forthcoming). Roscoe Pound and academic community on the Great Plains: The interactional origins of American sociological jurisprudence at the University of Nebraska, 1900-1907. In J. R. Wunder (Ed.), *Law, the Bill of Rights, and the Great Plains.*

Hill, M. R., & Deegan, M. J. (1991). Hattie Plum Williams (1878-1963). In M. J. Deegan (Ed.), *Women in sociology: A bio-bibliographical sourcebook* (pp. 440-448). Westport, CT: Greenwood.

Horowitz, I. L. (1983). *C. Wright Mills: An American utopian.* New York: Free Press.

Howard, G. E. (1904). *A history of matrimonial institutions chiefly in England and the United States* (3 vols.). Chicago: University of Chicago Press.

Illich, I. D. (1982). *Gender.* New York: Pantheon.

John Crerar Library. (1909). *The John Crerar Library: A list of books in the reading room.* Chicago: Board of Directors, John Crerar Library.

Kasler, D. (1981). *Methodological problems of a sociological history of early German sociology* [Photocopy]. Paper presented at the University of Chicago, Department of Education.

Kecskemeti, C. (1987). The professional culture of the archivist. *American Archivist, 50* (Summer), 408-413.

Keen, M. (1991). *The Freedom of Information Act and sociological research.* Department of Sociology, Indiana University, South Bend. Unpublished paper.

Kenworthy, M. A., King, E. M., Ruwell, M. E., & Van Houten, T. (1985). *Preserving field records: Archival techniques for archaeologists and anthropologists.* Philadelphia: University Museum, University of Pennsylvania.

Kurtz, L. R. (1984). *Evaluating Chicago sociology: A guide to the literature, with an annotated bibliography.* Chicago: University of Chicago Press.

Larsen, J. C. (Ed.). (1988). *Researcher's guide to archives and regional history sources.* Hamden, CT: Library Professional Publications.

Leinfellner, W. (1976). *Theory of human evaluation and decision making* [Mimeographed lecture notes]. University of Nebraska-Lincoln, Department of Philosophy.

Long, J. (1987). *Telling women's lives: The new sociobiography* [Photocopy]. Paper presented at the annual meetings of the American Sociological Association, Chicago, IL.

Martineau, H. (1989). *How to observe morals and manners* (sesquicentennial ed., with an introduction by M. R. Hill). New Brunswick, NJ: Transaction Books. (Original work published 1838)

Martineau, H. (1848). *Eastern life past and present.* London: Edward Moxon.

Martineau, H. (1864). *The history of England from the commencement of the XIX century to the Crimean War* (4 vols.). Philadelphia: Porter & Coates.

Martineau, H. (1869). *Biographical sketches.* New York: John B. Alden.

Marx, K. (1906). *Capital: A critique of political economy* (F. Engels, Ed.). New York: The Modern Library. (Original work published 1867)

Mead, G. H. (1899). The working hypothesis in social reform. *American Journal of Sociology, 5* (March), 367-371.

Mead, G. H. (1934). *Mind, self & society from the standpoint of a social behaviorist* (C. W. Moriss, Ed.). Chicago: University of Chicago Press.

Mead, G. H. (1936). *Movements of thought in the nineteenth century.* Chicago: University of Chicago Press.

Mills, C. W. (1959). *The sociological imagination.* New York: Oxford University Press.

Morgan, B. J. (Ed.). (1992). *Information industry directory* (12th ed.) (Vol. 1). Detroit: Gale Research.

Morris, A. D. (1984). *The origins of the civil rights movement: Black communities organizing for change.* New York: Free Press.

Nandan, Y. (1977). *Durkheimian school: A systematic and comprehensive bibliography.* Westport, CT: Greenwood.

National Historical Publications and Records Commission. (1988). *Directory of archives and manuscript repositories in the United States* (2nd ed.). Phoenix, AZ: Oryx.

Neier, A. (1975). *Dossier: The secret files they keep on you.* New York: Stein & Day.

Platt, J. (1981a). Evidence and proof in documentary research. I: Some specific problems of documentary research. *Sociological Review, 29* (February), 31-52.

Platt, J. (1981b). Evidence and proof in documentary research. II: Some shared problems of documentary research. *Sociological Review, 29* (February), 53-66.

Popplestone, J. A. (1975). Retrieval of primary sources. *Journal of the History of the Behavioral Sciences, 11*(1), 20-22.

Porter, D. S. (1981). The law of copyright relating to the photocopying of unpublished manuscripts. *Journal of the Society of Archivists, 6*(8), 493-497.

Post, J. B. (1983). Copyright mentality and the archivist. *Journal of the Society of Archivists, 8*(1), 17-22.

Quadagno, J. (1988). *Transformation of old age security: Class and politics in the American welfare state.* Chicago: University of Chicago Press.

Reinharz, S. (1984). *On becoming a social scientist* [With a new introduction by S. Reinharz]. New Brunswick, NJ: Transaction Books.

Reinharz, S. (1992). *Feminist methods in social research.* New York: Oxford.

Rhoades, L. J. (1981). *A history of the American Sociological Association.* Washington, DC: American Sociological Association.

Riesman, D. (1962). Law and sociology: Recruitment, training, and colleagueship. In W. M. Evan (Ed.), *Law and sociology* (pp. 12-55). New York: Free Press.

Ross, D. (1990). *The origins of American social science.* New York: Cambridge University Press.

Rule, J. B. (1974). *Private lives and public surveillance: Social control in the computer age.* New York: Schocken.

Schutz, A. (1970-1971). *Collected papers* (3rd unchanged ed.) (3 vols.). The Hague, The Netherlands: Martinus Nijhoff.

Schutz, A., & Luckmann, T. (1973). *The structures of the life-world.* Evanston, IL: Northwestern University Press.

Sheehy, E. P. (Ed.). (1986). *Guide to reference books* (10th ed.). Chicago: American Library Association.

Stanfield, J. H. (1985). *Philanthropy and Jim Crow in American social science.* Westport, CT: Greenwood.

Stanfield, J. H. (1987). Archival methods in race relations research. *American Behavioral Scientist, 30,* 366-380.

Stevenson, N. C. (1977). *Search and research.* Salt Lake City, UT: Deseret.

Stieg, M. F. (1988). Introduction to archival research. In J. C. Larsen (Ed.), *Researcher's guide to archives and regional history sources* (pp. 1-17). Hamden, CT: Library Professional Publications.

Strong, W. S. (1990). *The copyright book: A practical guide* (3rd ed.). Cambridge: MIT Press.

88

Thomas, W. I., & Znaniecki, F. (1918-1920). *The Polish peasant in America: Monograph of an immigrant group* (5 vols.). Chicago: University of Chicago Press.

Tissing, R. W., Jr. (1984). The orientation interview in archival research. *American Archivist, 47* (2, Spring), 173-178.

Turner, V. (1969). *The ritual process: Structure and anti-structure*. Chicago: Aldine.

U.S. Congress. (1977). *A citizen's guide on how to use the Freedom of Information Act and the Privacy Act in requesting government documents* (95th Congress, 1st Session, House Report No. 95-793). Washington, DC: Government Printing Office.

Urch, G. (1992, August 9). Seeing the world through Rachel's eyes. *Chicago Tribune*, section 6, p. 8.

Wall, C. E. (Ed.). (1971). *Cumulative author index for Poole's index to periodical literature, 1802-1906*. Ann Arbor, MI: Pierian.

Webb, E. J., Campbell, D. T., Schwartz, R. D., & Sechrest, L. (1966). *Unobtrusive measures: Non-reactive research in the social sciences*. Chicago: Rand McNally.

Weber, M. (1958). *The city* (D. Martindale & G. Neuwirth, Eds. and Trans.). Glencoe, IL: Free Press.

Weber, M. (1968). *Economy and society: An outline of interpretive sociology* (G. Roth & C. Wittich, Eds.) (3 vols.). New York: Bedminster.

Weber, M. (1985). *The protestant ethic and the spirit of capitalism* (T. Parsons, Ed., with an introduction by A. Giddens). London: Unwin Paperbacks.

Weinberg, J. (1972). *Edward Alsworth Ross and the sociology of progressivism*. Madison, WI: State Historical Society of Wisconsin.

ABOUT THE AUTHOR

MICHAEL R. HILL is an interdisciplinary scholar holding earned doctorates in both geography and sociology. His intellectual interests include theory, methods, institutions, the history of sociology, and the critical analysis of everyday life. His archival work includes service on the American Sociological Association's Committee on Archives and an ASA/NSF Problems of the Discipline Grant under which he inventoried the ASA's archival records at the Library of Congress. Hill's sesquicentennial edition of Harriet Martineau's *How to Observe Morals and Manners* excavates the earliest known methods text in sociology. He is the author of *Walking, Crossing Streets, and Choosing Pedestrian Routes* and *Women and Symbolic Interaction*. Currently teaching at the University of Nebraska-Lincoln, he has taught also at Albion College, Iowa State University, and the University of Minnesota-Duluth. Hill lives and writes in Nebraska and Michigan with his life-partner, Mary Jo Deegan, and their dog, Emma.